Statement

All facts and events described in this book are based on real-life experiences and personal recollections. While the essence of each story remains true, some names, locations, timelines, and identifying characteristics have been changed or omitted to protect the privacy of individuals and to prevent any potential legal issues.

Pseudonyms have been used where necessary. The intention of this work is not to harm, accuse, or defame any person, living or deceased, but rather to shed light on difficult truths, raise awareness about emotional and psychological abuse, and document the author's journey of healing and self-discovery.

The author acknowledges that memory can be imperfect and that others involved may have different interpretations of the same events. This book reflects her truth.

All profits from this book will go to a nonprofit organization in Brazil, founded by the author, to support individuals who cannot afford mental health treatment. This book was written to raise awareness of emotional abuse, codependency, and the invisible wounds left behind.

Cover Photography by Take it Photo.

Dedication

I dedicate this book to all the women who are able to rise and shine after enduring emotional abuse, to my parents, siblings and son who stood by my side through it all, to my friends, to my boss that recognized and acted when she sensed I needed help, and to my therapists, Paula and Maricay, who graciously held my hand throughout the process.

Author's Note

Who is Gabriela?

That's the question I've asked myself my entire life.
And this book is my answer.

I wrote this not to entertain, but to reveal.
To pull back the curtain on what emotional abuse looks like behind closed doors, when no one is watching. When the bruises are invisible, but the wounds run deep.
To show the world that it's not just fists that hurt. Words do too. Silence does too. Indifference, gaslighting, betrayal, they break you in ways that can't be seen on an X-ray.

This is not just my story. It's the story of so many women who've been told they were too emotional, too demanding, too much, when all they wanted was love, truth, and safety.

You may cry while reading this.
You may feel rage, grief, and even shame.
But if you're here, if you're reading these words, then you're already on your way to reclaiming your truth.

This book was my way out.
And I hope it becomes yours, too.

With love and truth,
Gabriela Fonseca

Table of Contents

Chapter 1: Who Is Gabriela 11
Chapter 2: Teenage Days 17
Chapter 3: The Dark Side Took Over 27
Chapter 4: My Greatest Gift 33
Chapter 5: The Best Years of My Life 41
Chapter 6: The One Who Was Good to Me 47
Chapter 7: The Beginning of an Imaginary Fairytale 53
Chapter 8: The First Year with the One I Thought Was My Forever 59
Chapter 9: Our First, the Illusion of Forever 63
Chapter 10: The Year the World Shut Down, and I Rose 69
Chapter 11: The House, The Wedding, and The Undoing *(Part 1)* 79
Chapter 11: The House, The Wedding, and The Undoing *(Part 2)* 95
Chapter 12: When the Ground Cracked and Swallowed Me Whole 119
Chapter 13: The Ruins Were Still Warm, and I Was Still Lying in Them 127
Chapter 14: A War I Never Asked For 133
Chapter 15: Even the Silence Was Loud 157
Chapter 16: The Illusion of Peace 161
Chapter 17: The Chains of Codependency 165
Chapter 18: The Women Who Helped Me Rise 203
Chapter 19: The War We Don't See: A Final Word on Emotional Abuse 207

Chapter 1: Who Is Gabriela

Well, this is all new to me.
And I don't know exactly where to begin, because…
How do you summarize a life that's felt like a roller coaster of love, loss, hope, rage, softness, strength, and chaos, all wrapped into one woman?

My name is Gabriela Fonseca, known as Gabby.
And for most of my life, I've felt like I've been searching, for stability, for love that doesn't hurt, for a safe place for my heart. For someone who sees me, not just a smile, not just a pretty face, not just a great career, not just the accomplishments, but me. The fun, messy, emotional, sensitive, fierce, loyal, brave, exhausted, hopeful me.

I was a very happy little girl.
I was born in Brazil, in Belo Horizonte. I came into this world on a Friday, why not? A Sagittarius. Half woman, half animal. That explains my "light-up-the-room" attitude. I was born to two very young, loving parents.
Obviously, I don't have many memories from that time, I was just an infant. But a year later, my sister came into the picture.
One-year-old Gabby didn't understand that.
And one-year-old Gabby began developing a distorted perception that she was being rejected.

My father came from a family marked by deep abuse, and while he was always loving in his own way, he never quite knew how to express it openly. My mother, on the other hand, was raised in a household with nine siblings, where affection was a rare luxury. My grandmother wasn't very affectionate, and although my mom loved us deeply, she too struggled to show it in ways a child might recognize. I was the kind of child who craved love, attention, and constant reassurance. And I believe that's where the idea of rejection first took root, somewhere in the mind of a one-year-old little girl who simply needed to feel seen, heard, and held.

So, when I think back, when I remember the little (well, not so little) beatings I gave my sister. the attitude, the lack of friendship between us even though we were just a year apart, after reading *Codependent No More* by Melody Beattie, I realized something. I wasn't just codependent on people. I was also living with a deeply rooted, distorted belief: that I was unworthy. That I was unloved and that I was rejected.

And the saddest part? I carried that with me for years... forty years.

After my sister was born, we moved to the United States. I was two. We lived there for a few years before moving back to Brazil when I was six.

Let me backtrack for a moment, my sister was born in a different city: Goiânia.

Our time in America was joyful, playful, warm. It felt like home to me.

But when we moved back to Brazil, everything shifted.

I remember being in school, not being able to say my ABCs. That moment, one of the first traumatic memories I hold onto. The whole class laughed at me. I ran out to the swing set and sat there until my dad came to get me. That's one of those moments that never leaves you.

I have great and horrible memories of my grandfather. He was loving, he used to sit me on his lap, play with his cigarette, burn little holes in napkins like it was some sort of magic trick. But he was also volatile. I remember him showing up to my grandma's house drunk on her birthday. My dad and uncle had to kick him out. He was emotionally and physically abusive, not just to them, but also to my grandmother.

But my dad? He chose the opposite.
He broke the cycle.
He became a man I am so proud of. An example. A protector. A father.

My grandma was the embodiment of love and warmth. She hand-painted her spare bedroom with such care and beauty just for me and my sister, making sure it felt like a place of magic and comfort. Even while living through her own version of hell, she never once let it show, not with her sons, and certainly not with us, her granddaughters and grandsons. What a woman she was. Gentle yet strong, selfless and full of grace. She raised my father to become the incredible man he is, and for that, I will forever honor her legacy.

A few years later, maybe I was seven or eight, I remember trying to celebrate my birthday. It's four days before Christmas, so school was already out for summer break in Brazil. I passed out my invites, excited, hopeful.
No one came.
Except for one girl, Martina.
She showed up toward the end with some candy. And I was happy, because once again, I was craving to be seen. That moment stayed with me, carving deeper into the beliefs I didn't even know I was forming.

Years later, I had my 15th birthday, what we call the "sweet 16" in America. My parents threw me a gorgeous, beautiful party. Everything I wanted. And yet… that voice in my head again: "These people don't really like you." "They're just here for the party."
I felt alone in a room full of people. That's what rejection can do to you; it makes you believe lies even in moments of joy.

Despite all those memories that brought me a deep sense of rejection, I also had beautiful moments and unforgettable opportunities. I went to Disney World at a very young age,

traveled with my family, and shared laughter-filled days with my brother and sister. There was joy. There was love. There was fun. But why does only the rejection stand out so vividly?
Because that's what cognitive distortions and distorted perception do.
Those deeply ingrained, automatic thoughts that tell you you're not enough, warp the way you see your life. And the result is a version of reality where the good becomes faint and the pain takes center stage. The bad becomes the loudest voice in your memory, while the good fades into a whisper you can barely hear.

Before I came back to America, I met a boy who lived in another city. His name was Renato. I thought it was love, maybe because I was just longing to feel wanted. I didn't even know what love truly was. But I gave him my innocence. I said goodbye to him, and I moved back to the U.S.

And people forget, maybe I forgot, that I was a happy girl. Radiant. Joyful. Full of dreams.
I believed in God. I believed in love so deeply.
I believed that if I gave enough, if I loved hard enough, sacrificed enough, proved myself enough, then maybe I'd finally be loved in return.
But life had other plans.

I've been broken.
I've been lied to.
I've been manipulated by people who claimed to love me.
I've had moments where I felt like the entire world was against me and and all I had left was a bag of meds, a broken heart, and a mind full of voices whispering, "Why aren't you enough?"
And still, I stood back up.

I've cried on the bathroom floor.
I've hidden panic attacks behind fake smiles.
I've gone to work while my soul was screaming.
I've loved people who didn't love me back the way I needed.

I've begged for clarity, for honesty, for commitment… and instead I got silence. I got betrayal. I was gaslighted into believing I was the crazy one.
But I'm not crazy.
I'm not weak.
I'm a woman who has endured more emotional trauma than most people can imagine, and I'm still here.

This book, these chapters, this story… it's not about revenge.
It's not about victimhood.
It's about truth.
It's about reclaiming my voice after years of being silenced.
It's about showing the world that even when a woman is emotionally destroyed, mentally shattered, spiritually drained, she can rise.
She can come back.
She can heal.

And as I begin this journey, I want to say something important:
My parents were young. I was the firstborn. They were learning. Kids don't come with a manual, and each family has their own dynamics.
I remember that whenever there was tension, silence would often follow. I have this vivid memory of sitting by the couch, tears streaming down my face, quietly wishing someone would say something, anything. It wasn't meant to hurt me. Looking back, I understand it was seen as a way to teach a lesson or create space. But little Gabby didn't understand that.
She just felt the distance.
And it left her feeling afraid and unseen.
She got terrified of silent treatments after that.

Now, at 40, I've come to understand something: I was also flawed. No parent is perfect. And the very things I hated, I sometimes repeated.
We'll get to the chapter when my son was born, but for context, I

remember being mad once when he did something wrong and telling him, "I'm going to disappear, and you'll miss me."
And little did I know... I would come to America and spend a year and a half apart from him.
I'm sure that left a scar. He tells me he understands, and I did it for the future I am able to provide him now, but I'm sure he will carry that throughout his life.

I used to hear that I was "difficult to shop with" because I always seemed to "need" something. But looking back now, I understand it wasn't really about the things themselves. It was about the feeling they gave me. A small way to feel special. To feel noticed. To feel like I mattered, even if just for a moment.

So yes, this story is mine.
But it's also about all of us who were misunderstood children, who became imperfect adults, still healing the echoes of our past.

I am Gabriela.
Not just someone's ex-wife.
Not a label. Not a diagnosis.
Not a tragic story or a girl who got left behind.
I'm a fighter. A mother. A dreamer.
I am a survivor of emotional abuse, abandonment, betrayal so deep it nearly erased me, but it didn't.

And if you're reading this, if you've ever questioned your worth because of how someone treated you...
If you've ever wondered if you were too much, or not enough, or if love is supposed to feel like pain, this is for you.

I am Gabriela Fonseca.
And I am here to tell it all, raw, honest, and unfiltered.

Chapter 2: Teenage Days

My teenage years were wild. Some of the best and worst moments of my life happened during that time.
They were messy, beautiful, chaotic, and they made me who I am.

Middle school was in Brazil. I went to a private school where there were two very clear groups: the pretty, popular kids, and the ones no one paid attention to, the quote-unquote rejected ones.
Naturally, I tried everything I could to fit in with the "cool" crowd. I started smoking cigarettes. I skipped school. I did everything I thought would make me feel accepted. But deep down, I never did. I always felt like I was standing on the outside, just watching. The truth is, I never really belonged. I don't even talk to most of those people today, and I don't I have any special memories with any of them.

I remember this one boy I liked, Pedro. My dad was going to the U.S., and I asked for an expensive Lacoste cologne, and he brought it back for me. And guess what? As we were flirting and I felt my heart warm around him, in an attempt to be accepted, loved, and seen, I gifted him that perfume. Did it make any difference? No. But in my distorted perception of reality, I believed it would bring him closer.

When we moved back to the U.S., I started high school at Spanish River High School. By then, I didn't remember much English since I'd spent most of my childhood in Brazil. I was placed in ESOL classes for students still learning the language. But I adapted quickly, I've always been good at surviving new environments, at reinventing the wheel.

Within a few days, I found myself gravitating toward the wrong crowd again. I remember one of my first days: the group I had just met decided to skip class. Since I used to do that in Brazil, I thought, "Why not?" But this wasn't Brazil. I went to the

bathroom, stepped on the toilet to hide, and I got caught. That's how I learned what detention was. But me being me, it was going to be an event. A water bottle filled with vodka got the whole room drunk, and I earned myself more detention and even some days picking up trash in the cafeteria.
Welcome to American high school.

In ESOL, I met Nicholas, an Argentinian boy who became my first boyfriend in the U.S. He was sweet. We had fun. It felt light. But I don't remember why we broke up. Maybe because kindness made me uneasy, and I didn't know what to do with something that didn't hurt. I thought I wanted to be loved, but every time it came close, I'd flinch. Because love, real love, felt unfamiliar. Almost threatening. I said I wanted to be loved, but deep down, love scared me. Rejection felt more familiar than affection.

Then came Mike. He was so cute. I'd seen him at school, but we actually met at a club while booty dancing, yes, that was a thing back then. I turned around, kissed him, and suddenly, the next day he was my boyfriend.

Only problem? I didn't speak much English, and he didn't speak Portuguese. Every time we hung out, we needed a translator. I remember being at my friend Mariana's house once, and he told me he had to leave "soon." I was so confused. "The sun?" I kept asking. "What about the sun?" He finally said "early," and then I got it.
The relationship didn't last, but the memory still makes me smile.

Mariana, one of the first friends I made here and, until this day, still my rock. She lived right across from my door, so we were always in each other's houses. She had two older sisters, Tatiana and Luana (not my chaos twin Luana). We were all very young, wild, and free. No strings. No bills. Just plain, simple joy.

For the next school year, I was transferred to Olympic Heights High School, and that's where the real stories start.

We had a group, BDP: Brazilians Don't Play.
That wasn't just our crew; it was also our street racing team. I drove a silver Eclipse, stick shift, inspired by *Fast & Furious*. I wore braids, blasted music, and lived for chaos.

That's when I met Gerardo, no, his name is not misspelled. He was Mexican. He was trouble. And I always gravitated toward trouble. Around that time, I had moved and met Natalia who became one of my really good friends. Unfortunately, that friendship was ruined when I caught her kissing Gerardo in the pool while I went to the restroom.

After that, I dated a boy named Tyler for a short while, nothing serious, he wasn't just a fling. There was something magnetic about him.

I had a crush on another boy, Mark, but back then he didn't give me any attention, so nothing happened, not at least until 2012.

But then came Robert.
Robert was different. He was kind. Gentle. He knew I wasn't a virgin and didn't care. He loved me for me. He respected me. Treated me with a gentleness I wasn't ready to trust.
And I destroyed it.
I cheated on him, with his best friend, and then with his worst enemy.
Every time I did something wrong, I told him. I didn't even try to lie. And this amazing man forgave me again and again.
Eventually, I started making excuses not to kiss him. "Your goatee bothers me," I said. I broke up with him without any real reason. He showed up outside my house, yelling, kicking his car. My sister begged me to go talk to him. I refused. I let him suffer.
Then one day, he cheated on me, with a girl named Bruna.
And that broke me.
For the first time, I felt what he must've felt.
I understood betrayal. I got mad. I yelled. But I forgave him. It

would've been hypocritical of me to not forgive a man I had failed to be loyal to, and to condemn him for the same behavior.

Then came spring break.
I had gone to Busch Gardens with my friend Desiree and a few other girlfriends whose names I, unfortunately, don't remember. Robert, driving with someone else, took my car to Tampa to come pick me up so we could head to Daytona Beach together. He always showed effort in our relationship. He always made me feel seen, loved, and respected.
On that same trip, for some reason, my sister wanted to come too. Since I always led the pack and there was no GPS back then, I drove back from Daytona, got into a major argument with my parents, who didn't want us driving late at night to somewhere so far. And nowadays, I get it, it was unnecessary, and we could have waited. But my mind was made up, and there was no changing it. I only drove back so she could follow me, and we headed back to Daytona together. One night, she accidentally rear-ended my car, not a serious crash, another ripple in the madness. We didn't even fight about it, just looked at each other and laughed. That was our rhythm: crash, chaos, and somehow… closeness.

Daytona was wild. Beads everywhere. One crowded room at Extended Stay America filled with laughter, music, and all our friends. I still have pictures in bed with Robert and a room full of people. Despite everything else going on in my life, that trip left me with one of the best memories from that time.

Robert and I stayed together for about a year, on and off. We had some fun in bed, but we never slept together. He was a genuinely good man, and somehow, I let my wounds sabotage what we had.

Then came my real first love.
I won't say his name, he knows who he is.
I've never loved anyone like I loved him, and if I'm entirely honest, not even my husband.
We were young, untamed, and perfect in our chaos, until I lost

him.
It felt easy. We quickly slept together, and he stole my heart and never gave it back.
I still remember our song, *Me Espera*, by Sorriso Maroto. When it plays, I still smile.

We were at a Brazilian party in a hotel, celebrating Carnival, until this day, I still have a newspaper clipping from that night.
Someone handed me a whippet canister. I didn't think twice. I fainted.
When I came to, I told him my blood pressure had dropped and rushed to the bathroom.
But the truth? I laughed about it with my friends, pretending it was no big deal, like I had fooled him.
He was only 14, but already so grounded. He didn't smoke, didn't drink, didn't do drugs. He played soccer, focused on his goals, and had a clear sense of what he stood for.
Someone overheard us laughing. Someone who wanted him. She told him what really happened.
He confronted me, calmly but firmly. Told me what he'd heard.
And just like that, he broke up with me.
He didn't yell. He didn't shame me. He simply chose his values over me.
And he was right.
He never hurt me. On the contrary, he offered stability and grace I had never truly known. But I made a choice, and choices come with consequences.
That was the end of what I thought was the beginning of forever.

After that, I unraveled.
I started drinking. Drag racing. Partying harder. I even got into fights, scheduled fights, which now I despise, and I am far from proud of. But it's part of my story.

I remember one fight where a girl named Monica (I'm so sorry) tried to help her friend who was already fighting with someone

else, but for some reason, I thought she was trying to jump in. I grabbed her, threw her on the floor, and hurt her badly. As I sat on her chest holding her arms down, my friend Vinny, known by everyone as Chocolate, sat in front of me and calmly said:
"Don't look down. Keep punching."
And I did.
Monica had braces. Her face was badly injured.
Then we heard the cops were coming. I jumped in my car and hid in a neighborhood. When things cooled down, I drove away like nothing happened.

Rest in peace, Vinny, Chocolate.
You died in a car accident way too young.
You were kind, loyal, and one of the few steady presences in my life.
I hope you're still watching over us.

Back then, I was fire, sharp, fearless, and untouchable on the outside. Cold eyes. Braided hair. Always surrounded by guys.
I walked the school hallways like I owned them. No one messed with me.
That was the persona I created, because I was falling apart underneath. I was confident, but at the same time, I was a mess. Skipping classes. Drinking. Running from cops. Trespassing neighborhoods. Smoking. You name it, I did it.

When I was a teenager, I developed this painful perception that every time I became close with someone, someone I really connected with, my sister would swoop in and claim them as her best friend. It wasn't always true, and maybe it wasn't even intentional, but that's how it felt to me. With rejection already rooted so deeply inside me, I didn't fight for those friendships. I didn't assert my place or see my sister as just another friend in the group. Instead, I backed off. I let go. I chose isolation over competition, even when there was no competition at all.
How twisted can a mind become when shaped by early wounds?

So twisted that it convinces you to retreat, even from love.
So twisted that it makes you feel like there's only ever space for one, and it's never you.

Some of my closest friends back then:

- Mariana, even though we fought over Robert, I was the bad one. She dated him first, and out of respect, I should have never dated him, but I did. Thankfully, our friendship was strong enough to withstand that, and here we are, 25 years later, still friends.
- Luana, my chaos twin. We were way too much trouble together, but irrelevant to this book.
- Lucas, Kinder Ovo, Ítalo, you were all part of my wild, unforgettable youth.
- And then there was Tamy. Sweet. Steady. Always there for me. In the next chapter, I'll talk more about her and just how much she meant to me, she saved my life.

The drinking and partying didn't stop.
One night, I drank an entire bottle of aguardiente with a coworker from the time I worked at JB's on the Beach, where I also met another really good friend, Dina.
We partied like nothing could touch us, naive, fearless, and dangerously unaware of our limits.

At some point, we drove to a gas station to buy cigarettes. I was so drunk, completely out of it, that I walked out without paying. He ran back inside to cover for me. By the time he came back to the car, I was out cold, fully unconscious. I had slipped into what I now know was an alcoholic coma.

How irresponsible are teenagers?
He took me to a friend's house and laid me on the couch.
I know for certain nothing sexual happened, because I would have felt it and known the next day, but the truth is, I could have never

woken up.
That could've been the end of me.
All because I didn't know how to cope, how to regulate, how to see my worth beyond the bottom of a bottle.

The next morning, he gently took me to my car, and that's when I woke up, in the driver's seat of my own car. He had put me there because he had to go to work.

And that's when I saw it:
Over 100 missed calls.
All from my dad.
He had called every hospital. Every fire station. Every place imaginable.
He thought I was dead.

I threw my phone into the back seat and still drove home drunk, disoriented, numb.
As I approached the neighborhood, I saw my dad leaving. I thanked God.
But little did I know… he turned around.
I was still drunk, sloppy, taking too long to get out of the car, and when I walked in, he pushed me against the wall.
I slid down.
He screamed and screamed.
Grounded me again. I was sick all day and all night, trying to throw up and not knowing what to do with myself.

I didn't care. I kept sneaking out, jumping out the window.
Eventually, my parents had enough.
I don't remember the final straw, but they kicked me out.

I moved in with my friend Lillian.
I was still heartbroken from losing the first boy I truly loved

I had no job.
I was 18.
I felt like I had no purpose.

And that's when I decided…
But that story, the darkest one of all, will begin in the next chapter.

Chapter 3: The Dark Side Took Over

I thought I had no purpose. At 18 years old, kicked out of the house, heartbroken, aimless, it felt like the world was ending. And that's when the dark side took over me.
I was staying at my friend Lillian's house. She was kind enough to take me in, but one night, she and her boyfriend were there, and she told me I'd need to find another place soon. That it was temporary.
And that's how far I had fallen. That's how alone I felt.

The memory from that night is blurry. But I remember the moment I decided. I decided it was time for me to go.
I drove to Walgreens, calmly picked up a bottle of Tylenol PM, and bought a small water bottle. I drove to the rocks by the beach at Lake Boca. And I swallowed all 50 pills, some with water, some dry.
At first, I just wanted to disappear. I didn't realize the full extent of what I was doing.
But my body didn't agree. I started feeling sick.
Panicked, I called my chaos twin, Luana. Somehow, I made it to her house. She helped me out of the car and put me in her bed. But my body was already shutting down.

The next thing I remember, it was already the afternoon of the next day.
The drugs had been in my system for nearly 24 hours. I was hallucinating. My body was giving up. I felt sick, disoriented, and heavy with the weight of what I had done.
And then I began to crawl.
I needed help. I was overdosing and dying.
I crawled from Luana's room all the way to her mom's bedroom and somehow pulled myself into her mother's bed.
That image is burned in my memory, me crawling like a ghost.

That evening, finally, came my angel.
Tamy walked into the apartment. She saw me and immediately knew something was wrong.
She asked, "What did you take?"
I couldn't speak. I just kept showing her five fingers. Over and over.
"Five?" she asked.
"No," I'd signal again.
Eventually, she added the fives together and realized I had taken fifty of something.
When she asked what it was, I finally said it.
Tylenol PM.

She didn't waste a second.
She helped me up, wrapped her arm around me, and together, we walked across the street to the emergency room.
God doesn't make mistakes.
Luana's house was right across from one of the best hospitals in the area.
Tamy told them what I had taken.
They asked me, "Why?"
And I said it: "I wanted to die."
They immediately Baker Acted me and rushed me back.

Charcoal intubation.
It wasn't technically intubation, but it felt like it. A tube down my throat while I was still awake, trying to pump charcoal into my stomach to save what they could.
I was gagging. Choking. But conscious.
It was the worst feeling ever.
That's the last thing I remember.

Then came the coma.
I don't know how long I was in the ICU. A week? Two? Three? The days vanished in a blur. Even now, I rarely speak about that time. It still feels too heavy, for me, and for my family.

What I do remember is this:
The doctors said I might not make it. That I wasn't coming out of the coma.
And I remember, clear as day, that they suggested removing me from life support.
That's something I've never really talked about with my parents.
Not because I don't remember.
But because I do.
And it's too painful to revisit with them.

And then... I woke up.
Because of a tummy ache.
Yes, you read that right.

A stomachache woke me up from a coma.
I ripped all the tubes from my body and ran to the bathroom with explosive diarrhea.

As insane and ironic as it sounds, shit brought me back to life.

I remember the nurses running in, the machines beeping, panic everywhere.
I opened the bathroom door, looked at them, and calmly said:
"I'm pooping."
And they smiled.
They called it a miracle.

I was moved to a different room, and I had a sitter outside the door because I had been Baker Acted.
It was an isolation room, double-doored.
I stayed in the hospital for what I believe was at least 20 days, maybe more.
Tylenol contains paracetamol, which is extremely toxic to the liver, so my liver basically melted.
That's why I had to stay so long, they were trying to stabilize my body.

Eventually, I was moved to a bigger room, and ironically, it was kind of beautiful.
Huge windows. Soft light.
And visits from the people who loved me.
Friends. Friends' mothers. Even McDonald's.

Thank you, Sammy, another good friend of mine, for sneaking in a McDonald's meal on the stairwell when nobody was watching.
I wasn't supposed to eat greasy food, but it made me feel alive. So, I ate it anyway.

But I'd be lying if I said everything about my recovery was comforting.
One of the biggest disappointments I felt during that time… was knowing that the man I loved back then never came to visit me in the hospital.
He told me he didn't agree with what I did.
He said he wouldn't support that kind of behavior.
.And he didn't.
That hurt deeply.
But strangely… it also made me admire him more.
Because even in the most emotional moment, he stood his ground.
He knew how to differentiate right from wrong.
And even though it broke my heart, I respected it.
So props to him.
He not only never did me wrong, he showed me that what I did was not a solution to any of my problems.

And then came the moment I thought I was going home.
I wasn't.

Instead, I walked out of that hospital in handcuffs, escorted by a police officer, and placed in the back of a squad car.
That was my walk of shame.
No one told me what was happening.
Because I had been Baker Acted, I was being transferred to a psychiatric facility for mandatory evaluation.

That place was a nightmare.
Filthy. Cold. Inhumane.
They treated us like animals.

It didn't make sense, how could someone who tried to end their life, because they were so lost and broken, be placed in a facility that felt like a punishment?
It felt like jail, filled with drug addicts, people who needed help but were instead judged and mistreated.

But that's what happened.
Eventually, my parents stepped in and signed the paperwork to release me into their care.

My dad said, "Let's go back to Brazil."
And I agreed.

I'm not sure if I went right away or if some time passed.
I do remember that at some point, before or after, my parents moved back to Brazil and left me living alone in the U.S.
Later, they came back.

It's all jumbled now, memories from 25 years ago.
But I do believe it was before, because I had an accident at home and needed stitches… and Robert came to my rescue.

But I do remember this:
I ended up in Brazil.
And I never sought real help.
I just acted like nothing had happened.

No therapy. No real healing. Just survival.

I moved in with my aunt Adriana and my cousins, Marcela, Paula, and Bruno.
They were, and still are, a big part of my life.
Marcela especially gave me the support I needed when I had nothing.
She introduced me to people.

To friends.
To new places.

And that's when I met someone, I thought would be special.
He ended up giving me the greatest gift of my life.
But we'll get to that.

I started dating a boy named Marcelo.
Once again, I was bubbly. Happy. Traveling. Living.
And the next chapter will be about him… about us… about what came next.

Chapter 4: My Greatest Gift

I met Marcelo at a party.
I still have the picture from that night. I don't remember the name of the place or all the details, but I remember the connection.
We clicked right away. It was effortless.

And just like that, we started seeing each other, and before I even realized it, I was in a new relationship.

It felt deep. Maybe because I had never really healed.
I had never truly processed what I had lived through. I hadn't gone to therapy. I hadn't explored the roots of my trauma. I hadn't learned about codependency, about emotional triggers, or how deeply my perception of rejection had been distorted.
Back then, I thought I was seeing things clearly.
But I was still viewing life through a shattered lens.

We had so much fun together. I'd skip college classes just to spend time with him. It got serious fast, and we started making plans. I was going to return to the U.S. to get everything in order so we could build a life together.

And I did. I came back and stayed for thirty days.
But the distance felt unbearable. I missed him too much.
So, I flew back to Brazil. We tried to get him a visa in Rio, but of course, he was young, with no formal ties to prove stability, it was denied in under twenty minutes.

Back then, everyone was using Fotolog, that early version of social media where we shared pieces of our lives in pixels and captions. One day, while scrolling, I saw a picture that made my stomach drop.

It was him.
In the background.
Lying on a couch with a girl's head resting on his lap.

And me being Gabby...
I did what any Latina woman with intuition would do.
I investigated.

Because when we want the truth, we don't stop until we find it.

And I found it.

He was cheating on me.

That discovery broke something in me.
I fell apart. I called him nonstop. Reached out to his friends. I begged. I cried. I spun out.

But truthfully, I had already been unraveling long before that.

The pain that brought me to Brazil in the first place, the suicide attempt, the heartbreak, the trauma, none of it had been addressed. My parents were doing the best they could, trying to navigate something none of us truly understood.
And back then, there weren't Instagram therapists or Google search bars offering instant answers about trauma, attachment styles, or mental health.

It was just survival.

I fell into a deep depression.
A psychiatrist prescribed medication.
And somewhere in that chaos, while we were not quite broken up, not quite together, I got pregnant.

And then, God stepped in.

At the time, I weighed barely 40 kilograms.
When the doctor confirmed my pregnancy, I'll never forget what she said:
"I don't even know how this happened. Your body shouldn't be able to sustain a pregnancy."

But it did.
It did.

My pregnancy was far from easy.
The first sixty days were a blur of debilitating migraines, and I didn't have much support from him. I remember sitting on a curb, waiting for him to pick me up for an ultrasound.
He never came.

My parents took me.
That scene repeated itself throughout the pregnancy, I waited, and waited, and was left disappointed.

My father, despite his frustration, stepped into action. He gave Marcelo a job to help him step into fatherhood, to carry his responsibilities with dignity.
But instead, he got a new cell phone and a tattoo on the back of his leg.

Then came April 16, 2006.

The best day of my life.

The day my son was born.
Vitor Fonseca, my greatest blessing, my best friend, my reason to keep going.

But even that day was not without its shadows.

During my pregnancy, I had already discovered Marcelo was cheating.
I met the first girl. She looked at my growing belly, apologized, said she hadn't known. Said she never meant to come between us. And still… it didn't stop there.

Another girl came after her.
A different betrayal.

On the day Vitor was born, Marcelo arrived late.
He was late because he'd been dropping that second girl off.

Even then, I asked the doctors to wait.
I didn't want them to begin the C-section until he arrived.

Because even after everything, I wanted him there to witness his son's first breath.

I waited too long.
And because of that delay, I ended up feeling the pain,
the scraping of the placenta from inside my body.
The pain was physical, yes, but the emotional weight of that moment… it cut even deeper.

I had waited for someone who didn't value the moment like I did.
And yet… even through all of that, my baby was here.
This radiant, innocent, beautiful child.
So full of sweetness and light.
So pure, he made me want to protect him from every wound I had ever carried.

That first year as a mother was a blur of diapers, sleepless nights, and this fierce kind of love I had never felt before. I didn't always know what I was doing, but I knew I would never let him feel unwanted. I may have been young, scared, and broken in many ways, but I showed up. Every single day. And somehow, that made me feel strong.

We tried to make it work for a few more months, but eventually, I had one of those moments I've learned to pay attention to now.

A shift. That quiet, inner click. A truth I couldn't unsee.

We broke up.

I remember running into him at a gas station later. He tried to talk to me.
I didn't want to hear it.
He tugged at my purse. It ripped.
He tried to follow me, crashed into or nearly crashed into a metal dumpster, I can't remember exactly.
But I do remember the elevator.
He looked at me, asked me for a kiss.

And I said:
"Abso-fucking-lutely not."

From there, things got legal.

We were both still so young, barely in our twenties. Broke.
We depended on our families.

I went to court and asked for structured visitation.
The judge ruled he would visit every weekend for a year to build a bond, and after that, we'd alternate weekends. I had full custody.
He signed child support, but let's just say... not all signatures translate into effort.
Vitor deserved more. He always has.

During that first year, he showed up a few times.
I was fiercely protective. I didn't want my baby out of my sight.
He was my sunshine. The only space in my life where rejection wasn't creeping in.

I remember one day, my sister took him to McDonald's with Marcelo.
I was livid when I found out.
The visits were supposed to be supervised, at home.
They came back, but we fought, he dropped Vitor off and walked away.

Eventually, we moved to a condo outside Belo Horizonte, in Alphaville.
He visited once or twice.
Vitor gave him tough assignments, requests for made-up toys and gifts that didn't even exist.
Me? I would've made them from scratch.
But Marcelo slowly disappeared.

Time passed.
The bond was never built.

But people change.
And I truly believe that today, he understands.
That he sees it differently now.
That he forgives himself.
Because the truth is, he was a kid too.
Unprepared. Unsupported.
And despite it all, he gave me the greatest gift of my life.

After Vitor was born, I felt whole.
No more panic attacks.
No depression.
No anxiety.
Just purpose.

Or maybe… maybe I became codependent again.
Perhaps I put all my joy into one person.
Maybe I expected my baby to heal everything I hadn't.

But he did something I never expected.
He saved me.

Vitor was born on Easter Sunday.
And he brought me back to life.

He knows everything about me.
He's not just my son, he's my confidant.
And I'm his.

I'm so proud of who he's become.
Polite. Kind. Grounded. Humble. Loyal.
Loving toward his girlfriend. Unafraid to be gentle.
Anchored in faith.

I went to hell and back.
And God gave me a miracle.

My one and only child.
My light.
My Vitor.

Chapter 5: The Best Years of My Life

It's hard to pack this chapter into one single storyline, because it spans nearly a decade.
My college years. My twenties.
Some of the best years of my life.

I was finally free.
Healed enough to laugh again.
Wild enough to live without apology.
And for the first time… I was surrounded by the best kind of people.

I started college when I was still pregnant with Vitor. After he was born, I took a short break, just six months. When I returned, everything changed. I met the women who would become my soulmates: Samyra, Tathi, Talita, Nunu, Ana Laura, and Bruna.

My rocks.
My flowers.
My sisters.

These girls weren't just party companions, they were home.
We shared our lives. Our beds. Our noodles. Our beer. Our laughter. Our heartbreaks.
We lived it all, together.

We started at hole-in-the-wall bars, drinking two-liter bottles of beer like they were water.
Our first Carnival together was in Diamantina, and it was pure magic.
We crammed into a tiny apartment where the shower was literally over the toilet. We lived on noodles and alcohol and belly-aching laughter.
And we made memories that still make my heart ache in the best way.

The next year? We did it again. Same chaos. Different stories.

By then, I had blossomed into a social butterfly.
I wasn't afraid of rejection anymore. I had found my people. My rhythm. My courage.

Between Carnivals were countless nights out.
Chalezinho, the original one, not the new location, became our haven.
We danced at clubs. Took spontaneous road trips.
One year, I had no plans for Carnival, and out of nowhere, I jumped in a car with my friend Rafael and drove to Diamantina.
We slept in the car like it was a five-star hotel.
I don't even remember where we showered, or if we did.
We didn't care.
We were free.

That season of my life was the longest I'd ever gone without a serious relationship. Seven, maybe eight years of total freedom. Barbara and I would travel to Rio and stay at our friend Bruno's place.
Betania, my amazing friend from the U.S., would fly in and we'd hop into hostels and go full tourist-mode, dancing until sunrise, meeting strangers, living unapologetically, beautifully.

I even ended up on stage with Flo Rida in Brazil during one of those wild nights, with Lorena, of course.
That clip still lives on YouTube.
And so does the memory.

Now, Lorena... where do I even begin?

If I told every story involving her, she'd probably kill me. But damn, they were epic.

We used to drive to rodeo-style shows in random cities and let loose like no one was watching. We drank, we danced, and yes, sometimes we made reckless choices.
Like drinking and driving. Something I'm not proud of and will

never condone.
But I'd be lying if I said God didn't assign us our own personal guardian angels.

One time, some guy at a bar made a disgusting comment to Lorena about her lipstick, called her a whore.
I blacked out with rage.
Ran toward him and drop-kicked him in the chest.
Yes, a literal flying kick.
The guy hit the floor. Chaos erupted.
People jumped in. It turned into a full-blown brawl.

Hours later, I was still drinking at a bar in the freezing morning air.
Lorena and my sister were begging to go home.
I looked at them and said, "Guess what? Now y'all really going to be cold."
Then I blasted the AC, rolled the windows down, and froze with them just to be petty.

I'm not proud.
But it's funny now.

We even had a *point system*.
Yes, a literal scoreboard. If you know, you know.
Let's just say… I won most of the time.
Lorena and my sister still try to argue that. But facts are facts.

And confidence? I had plenty.

I've always had that spark.
If I wanted someone, I'd stare them down until they came over.
And if they didn't? I'd walk right up and start the conversation myself.

My friends were always amazed by that.
I didn't miss. If I wanted something, I found a way to make it mine.
There was love, sex, adventure, confidence.

And if I'm being honest… I had the best twenties anyone could ask for.

Eventually, my sister moved back to the U.S. She spent a year there before we went to visit her during Christmas. That trip changed everything.

My dad sat me down and said, "If you want to build your career in America, I'll support you. You'll stay here, get your credentials. I'll take Vitor back with us until you're settled."

That was the plan.

What I should've completed in six months took me a year and a half.

Why?
Partying.
Distractions.
Boys.
Fun.

I was working two jobs, Vilagio during the day, and Bamboo nightclub at night.
At Bamboo, partying was part of the gig. So, I drank, danced, networked, flirted.

We'd finish work and head to Space or a strip club, yes, technically there are strippers, but really it was just the after-hours scene.
The girls there? Most of them were broken.
Using drugs just to keep going.
Some sold their bodies.
Not because they wanted to, but because survival demanded it.

I'd get home at 6, sometimes 7 a.m., sleep for an hour or two, pop an Adderall, and head straight to Vilagio for my morning shift.

I was burning the candle at both ends.
And through it all, my son was in Brazil.

I should've brought him sooner.
Should've finished faster.
There were nights I cried myself to sleep. But I wore my freedom like armor, pretending I wasn't bleeding underneath.

But I'll never pretend those years didn't matter.
They shaped and taught me.
And I believe, everything happens exactly as it's meant to.

Somewhere in the middle of that chaos, I reconnected with Mark, the boy I crushed on in high school.

It was a terrible relationship.
He was deep into drugs, and at one point, I even started using with him.

I wanted it to work.
I feared rejection, and I was still chasing healing in all the wrong places.
So I did what I always did, I overcompensated.

On his birthday, I could barely afford rent, but I bought him a Gucci wallet.

We were never "official," but somehow, we were.
He hurt me deeply.
Thankfully, I wasn't in love enough to stay broken.

Eventually, I snapped.
Flew to Brazil.
Spent a month with my son.
Recharged.

Came back ready to get my paperwork done.
Ready to get my life back on track.

At Vilagio, stories were endless, but a few stood out.

There was Gary, who sang to me at Dubliner karaoke after work. It made me feel special, but not enough to stay.

Then came Douglas, a short chapter, no strings attached.
And then... Yes, *that* one. The YouTuber.

We hooked up.
But I met him through his best friend, Patrick.
He worked with me.
We became inseparable.
Best friends. My person during that chapter of my life.

And that story...
belongs to the next chapter.

Chapter 6: The One Who Was Good to Me

Patrick.
That name carries a strange mix of peace and guilt. Peace, because he never hurt me, never lied, never manipulated, never abandoned me. And guilt, because maybe that's exactly why I couldn't fully accept him.
It's ironic how we sometimes chase the ones who destroy us and push away the ones who offer us safety.

We met at Villagio, both of us waiters, both tired from double shifts and dealing with difficult guests. But we laughed through the chaos. He had this calm-under-pressure energy that somehow matched my fire, it made no sense, but it worked.

We clicked instantly. No drama. No tension. Just something real. His wit was quick, his humor subtle, and there was an old-school charm to him that made you feel truly seen. Not watched. Seen. There's a difference. And I think he was one of the first to really see me.

He found out I worked at Bamboo, the nightclub, and showed up one night. That small gesture felt like everything. He came for me. And maybe that mattered so much because, deep down, I was still craving the feeling of being chosen.

From then on, it became routine. After our shifts at Villagio, we'd head to Dubliner. A few drinks. Conversations that flowed like water. Then off to Nippers for pool, I was good at it. Still am. There was something about those nights that made everything else disappear. The stress. The noise. The confusion. It all melted away in the rhythm of the game, the laughter, the glances.

It was simple. And I craved simple.
He made me feel special just by being impressed that I could kill it driving a stick shift.

He introduced me to one of his friends, the same one I mentioned in the last chapter. One night started at O'Brian's and spiraled into one of those chaotic, blurry, unforgettable evenings that ended at 7 a.m. at Scarlett's. I left with, ended up at Mariana's house, thinking something spontaneous and fun might happen, but his friends came to pick him up. He flew back to L.A. the next day. We exchanged a few texts, nothing serious. Still, I remember looking forward to his return.

Meanwhile, Patrick and I were growing closer. One night, after drinks, he walked me to my car. As I turned to say goodbye, he gently grabbed my face and kissed me. I pulled back, surprised. "What are you doing?" I asked. He looked embarrassed but honest. He told me he was starting to feel something for me.

I don't know if he ever told his friend about how he felt. But when his friend came back, he didn't give me any attention. I felt invisible. Maybe it was my distorted perception but I felt discarded, replaced like I didn't matter. And then he got involved with one of the hostesses. A girl who had a boyfriend. I felt small, confused, caught between wanting to be wanted… and wanting to disappear.

But Patrick... Patrick was steady.
Always kind. Always present. Always patient.

He was smart, funny, generous and he showed up. Again, and again.
Eventually, I let my guard down. I gave in. We started dating.

And it was easy. It was peaceful. It was safe.

He gave me what I didn't know I needed: calm. Stability. Ease. He didn't try to control me. He celebrated me. He encouraged my freedom to go out, see my friends, live my life. No guilt. No possessiveness.

He took my son out on little dates, just the two of them. He made it feel normal, warm… like we were a family.

He laughed with my friends. He danced with my chaos. There was no jealousy, no mind games, no toxicity. It was, by all definitions, the healthiest relationship I had ever known.

His family welcomed me like their own. His mom especially, what a woman. Warm, kind, loving. She treated me like a daughter, and I felt it.

But here's the part that still hurts to admit:
I don't think I ever truly loved him.

I loved the stability. I loved the kindness. I loved the feeling of finally being loved the right way. But love, real, deep, soul-level love? I don't think I gave that to him. I think I was with someone who finally gave me what I had always asked for... and I didn't know how to receive the very thing I had prayed for.

Because when you grow up starving, being fed feels overwhelming.

Sometimes he wanted more intimacy than I did. He wanted closeness. I'd pull away. Then I'd feel guilty.

How does someone who fears rejection... become the one who rejects love?

But that's what trauma does. It wires you backward. It tells you to run from what you've begged for. It confuses safety for boredom and chaos for passion.

Looking back with clarity, I know this now: Patrick wasn't "too much." He was exactly what I needed. But to the broken version of me, his consistency felt like discomfort. His love felt like too much, too soon because I was used to being starved for affection, not fed with it.

And I was always honest with him. I never cheated. I never lied. I never disrespected him.
I just couldn't give him my whole heart. I gave him what I could.

And he warned me. Every time we argued, he'd say, "You're going to end up with someone who's always busy, who puts you second, and who hurts you." He didn't say it to scare me. He said it calmly. Like he was just trying to protect me, from myself.
And he was right.

Eventually, he left for a 30-day trip to his home country. He called and texted almost daily, just to say he missed me. When he got back, I surprised him with a cruise. It was beautiful, but I realized: being stuck on a boat for days didn't feel like freedom. It felt like stillness and, I wasn't ready for stillness yet.

After that, life shifted. I left Villagio. I focused on my career. I started studying. I partied less. And with that, my feelings for him began to fade. Not because of anything he did. But because I was changing, and he no longer fit into the new version of me.

I stayed longer than I should've, two years, because it was easy. Because it was kind. Because I was afraid of breaking someone who had done nothing wrong.

But I did anyway.
I picked fights. Created chaos. He stayed calm, tried to understand me, held space. And I pushed him away. I confused peace for emptiness. And when he didn't give me the pain I was used to, I didn't know how to stay.

Ironically, and maybe this is one of the hardest truths I've had to face while writing this book:
In that relationship, I was the one who did the hurting.

Not intentionally. Not maliciously. But through my wounds, my reactivity, my unhealed patterns. I projected pain onto someone who didn't deserve it. I lashed out. I belittled. I shut down. I withheld affection and pushed him away, even when all he ever did was try to love me.

And that's the thing about trauma, it doesn't always make you the victim. Sometimes, it turns you into someone you don't recognize.

Someone who hurts others without meaning to. Someone who confuses peace for emptiness and pushes away the very thing they prayed for.

I emotionally exhausted him.

And I forgot something the world always reminds you of eventually:
It goes around.
And it always comes back.

Sometimes fast. Sometimes… about nine years later.

Patrick deserved better.
He deserved a woman who could love him the way he loved me: with clarity, consistency, and care.

He was the one who was good to me.
And to my son, who cried more for that breakup than I did.

Because he had loved Patrick, too.

Chapter 7: The Beginning of an Imaginary Fairytale

May 2015. I was still dating Patrick, a kind soul, a gentle man who called me "doll" and "princess." He brought me breakfast in bed almost daily, treated me with care, and made me feel safe. He was good. So good, in fact, that to this day, I've never spoken poorly of him. He didn't break my heart. I broke his. I just didn't know it at the time, blinded by the distorted perception I had of love.

That month, I went out with a friend to celebrate someone's birthday. Liv Nightclub. Loud music, packed crowd. I wasn't looking for anything. I had a boyfriend. But that night, I was introduced to a man, a stranger whose energy made me uncomfortable. Not because he did anything wrong, but because something inside me shifted. I knew someone was waiting for me at home, and yet... I felt pulled. I quickly walked away and didn't give him any attention. I went home to the man who waited for me in bed.

A year passed.

April 2016. Boca Bash. Daylight. Boats, champagne, sunburned skin, and loud music. I went with a friend and her then-husband. My boyfriend came too, but we weren't in a good place anymore.

And there he was, the same man from Liv. For legal reasons, we'll call him Ricardo. He tossed beads around my neck. Sprayed champagne across my body like I was in a music video. It was wild, playful, and part of me laughed. My boyfriend didn't seem bothered. He trusted me. He thought it was harmless.

But it wasn't harmless.

I should've known then that being objectified would become a pattern. But I mistook it for attention.

Later that day, after an argument and the frustration of losing one of my rings, I sat quietly at the edge of the boat. Disconnected. And that's when Ricardo and I started talking. The man I couldn't forget. The man I would end up marrying. The man I would spend the next nine years with.

I went home, but something lingered. I couldn't stop thinking about him. I felt torn, emotionally detached from the man who loved me and drawn to someone I barely knew. My boyfriend and I had a trip planned to Punta Cana. Little did I know how symbolic and destructive that place would become.

We went - me, him, and my guilt. I hadn't cheated, but my heart had drifted elsewhere. I drank too much to numb myself and avoided intimacy. I leaned on a friend who worked at the resort, trying to escape. My boyfriend sensed it. On the last day, in the hotel lobby, he confronted me. I took a breath, and I ended it. He didn't believe me. On the flight home, he still tried to hold on. But it was gone.

When we landed, he walked me to my car, like he always did. A man who used to leave red flowers tucked under my windshield wipers just to brighten my day. But that day, there were no flowers. Just confusion in his eyes and a quiet hope that maybe I didn't mean what I said.

"I'm sorry," I told him. "We're not together anymore. It's time you understand that."

I got in my car and drove away.

A few days later, I told my girlfriend I couldn't stop thinking about Ricardo. And the universe, or something more twisted, stepped in. Ricardo saw her pulling out of her complex, flagged her down, and asked for my number. She gave it to him. A few days later, he texted me. By Friday, we had our first date, exactly one week after I'd landed from Punta Cana.

He picked me up, opened the car door, acted like a gentleman. We drove to Miami to avoid being seen by anyone we knew. Dinner at The Forge. Tequila to ease the nerves. He was charming, but serious. I talked too much, as I always do. He listened, or at least pretended to.

After dinner, we walked to Rockwell. He called a promoter friend, and we were taken to a VIP table. A bottle of vodka. We danced. We drank too much. We laughed too loudly. At one point, I slipped, and as he caught me, he whispered, "I wanted to sweep you off your feet... literally." Then he kissed me.

Later that night, he handed his keys to the valet... even though we had walked there. I sat on the curb, laughing quietly to myself. I walked over and whispered, "We walked here." He grabbed his keys, apologized, and we took a yellow cab back to the Fontainebleau. He got us a room at 5 a.m. Saturday morning. I made it clear: "I don't sleep with clothes, but we're not doing anything." He respected that. I undressed and went to bed. He laid next to me, and that was it.

The next morning, I had a brutal migraine. I hadn't brought my meds, and when he realized how bad it was, he rushed to get dressed and take me home. We took another cab, wandered Washington Avenue searching for his lost car, eventually found it, and before we parted ways, he reminded me the hotel room was ours for another night. Did I want to go again?

I did.

That night, we met up with his best friend and went to Basement. More dancing, more drinking. We went back to the hotel. Again, I undressed. Again, nothing happened. But this time, he needed help taking off his clothes. He could barely stand.

It took about three weeks before I finally slept with him. And when I did, it was electric.

We texted constantly. Flirting became routine. One night, he invited me out with friends from Indiana. We were supposed to go to Tootsie's. We even matched our outfits, down to the shoes. On the way there, he found out about an ex I had dated at 18. My first real love.

He ghosted me for a week.

Now I see it: jealousy. Insecurity. Maybe even shame. That ex was well-known, handsome, desired. It threatened him.

But eventually, he came back. They always do.

We spent Fourth of July at the sandbar in Delray. It was the first time he asked me to take a photo together and post it. Looking back, it wasn't about romance. It was about marking territory. Letting my ex see that I was no longer available. Anyhow, we drank too much, got playful, and I lost his Gucci hat. Too drunk to drive, we sat on a bench and waited to be picked up. His mom came. That's how I met her. Embarrassed doesn't begin to cover it.

That night, we made love. He shouted, "I love you." I wasn't sure I heard it right, so I said nothing and kept going.

The next day, he casually mentioned the lost hat. I didn't flinch. I ordered a new one immediately. I was determined to prove I could be "worth it."

Another night, at Salt, my ex was there. Ricardo saw him, walked over, shook his friend's hand in front of him, then picked me up and carried me across the street. It was theatrical. Territorial. Disrespectful. And I regret allowing it.

Time passed. Mariana's birthday came, and she got drunk at Salt's brunch, said some things to both of us. But we were already wrapped up in each other.

Eventually, I asked if we were even a couple. I was tired of the guessing. He said we were. So, June 10th became our anniversary, the night of our first date.

Barbara G., my sister in every sense but blood, pulled me aside. "This man is no good. He's always in strip clubs, and I hear he's into shady business." Her words shook me. She never spoke without purpose.

I confronted him. He admitted the strip clubs but promised to stop if it made me uncomfortable. As for the rest, he brushed it off. Said Barbara was jealous. Toxic. From that moment on, he hated her. And I… pulled away from her. My first mistake.

We took trips. First to Bimini with his family. Then to Colorado to visit his brother. That trip gave me a false sense of stability. He held my hand. Made me laugh. Showed me a message he sent to an old flame, telling her he was in a relationship. I felt secure.

He started doing little things like paying security to escort me to the bathroom in clubs, buying me flowers. He loved me, or loved the version of me he could parade.

At one point, we went to a paintball tournament. We stayed at a cheap, sketchy motel, but I made the best of it. We played pool at a bar. I held back my skills and still crushed it.

On our six-month anniversary, he surprised me with six red roses and dinner at The Forge, our first date spot. Our song "Controlla" played during dessert. It felt like a movie.

Two weeks later, for my birthday, he decorated his house with balloons and streamers. Left a teddy bear and a pair of Louboutins waiting for me. He knew how to craft a moment.

Then came our first family trip to Las Vegas.

Before the airport, we stopped at his dad's house. My son was playing with Nerf guns with his little brother. One dart hit Ricardo in the eye. He snapped. Yelled at my son, harshly.

I stepped in. "You don't talk to my child like that," I told him. "That's not your place."

Tension filled the air. In Vegas, it got worse. He tried to bond with my son, but mostly, he was focused on finding weed. He's addicted and he can't function without it. It's how he copes with the trauma of his childhood. But I didn't understand it at the time.

I begged him to stop, just for a few days. He wouldn't. Eventually, he threw away his vape pen, but the damage was done. The mood was off. The energy changed.

It was our first trip as a family. And I already felt like I was suffocating. Like I was loving someone who needed control more than connection. Who loved me loudly, but only on his terms.

Behind the sparkle, something darker was brewing.

I thought I was being swept into a fairytale.

But I was only being pulled into a trap, one stitched together with charm, chaos, and control.

This was the beginning of an imaginary fairytale.

Chapter 8: The First Year with the One I Thought Was My Forever

It started like a fairytale, the kind you dream about as a little girl. The kind that feels almost too good to be real. The kind that makes you believe, even for a moment, that maybe all the pain and disappointment you've carried your whole life were just steppingstones leading you to the one.

That's what I thought this was.

From the beginning, he had a way of pulling me in. There was a mystery about him, a charm that felt both dangerous and magnetic. He didn't chase me like the others or flatter me with compliments. Instead, he watched, studied me. And that kind of attention, made me feel special. Like he saw something in me no one else had taken the time to notice.

And maybe that's where the hook was set. Because when you've been starving for real connection, even the smallest taste can feel like a feast.

He wanted to be close, but also distant. And I didn't feel rejected by that. I mistook it as just part of who he was.

The first year with him was intense. The highs were euphoric. The lows, I brushed off as normal. Every relationship has growing pains, right? Every couple has their moments.

I began to mold myself into the version of me I thought he would want. I silenced my intuition. I over-explained.
Conversations that once came easily, I now tiptoed around.

And whenever he pulled away, I leaned in harder.

Back then, I didn't understand relationship dynamics the way I do now. I didn't know about attachment styles. I didn't know that his avoidant attachment and my anxious one were the perfect storm.

Here's what I've come to understand:
Anxious lovers crave closeness. Reassurance. Connection. They fear abandonment and are hyper-aware of tone shifts, distance, or silence.
Avoidant lovers fear being overwhelmed. They crave independence and space. When things get too emotionally intense, they pull away, shut down, or detach.
One chases. The other flees.
And the tragedy is, they're both acting from fear.
One fears being left.
The other fears being trapped.

Without healing, this dynamic creates a loop, a dance of rejection, longing, and emotional starvation. It's a cycle neither can escape without deep self-awareness and growth.

I thought those traits meant he was complex, that there was more beneath the surface.
I confused distance for depth. Silence for strength. Possessiveness for passion.

But I couldn't see that then. I was caught in a story I had already written, the story where I finally found someone who would stay. Someone who would choose me. Build a life with me.

We went places. Took photos. Smiled in public. People called us the perfect couple, a power couple. And I clung to that image like it was proof. Proof that I was happy. That I was enough.

He'd say things that left me spinning. One day, I was the woman of his dreams. The next, he was cold, withdrawn, detached. And I would internalize the shift. Try harder. Love more. Shrink myself, just to be enough.

I blamed my anxiety. My past. My wounds.

Never him. Never his behavior.

Sometimes I'd surprise him and put on a sexy lingerie, trying to reignite something between us and he'd look at me and scoff, "What are you doing?" Like my efforts were embarrassing. Pathetic.

That was the beginning of my addiction to the cycle. The highs. The lows. The craving for connection that always felt just out of reach. I kept telling myself it would get better. That he just needed time. That love would be enough.

But deep down, something in me already knew.

This wasn't love.

It was survival dressed up as romance. It was codependency, disguised as destiny.

And I didn't see it yet.

I thought I had found my forever.
And maybe I had...
Just not in the way any little girl dreams of.

Chapter 9: Our First, the Illusion of Forever

In the beginning, and even throughout the nine years, there were many good memories. I'm not trying to erase those. They are years of my life, and they shaped me into a wiser, stronger woman. I truly believe God wouldn't have given me a burden this heavy if He didn't know I could carry it. But now, with the clarity I've gained, I realize that what I once considered "normal" was anything but. The behavior I tolerated, the emotional absence I accepted, it wasn't love, it was survival. He never made any real effort to be part of my world. My friends, my family, he kept them at arm's length. It was always about his people, his friends.

Little by little, it seemed like every friend I had become a problem. If it wasn't them directly, it was their boyfriends. He always had something negative to say, this one was jealous, that one was fake, the other was toxic. One of my friends was dating a cop, but apparently, he was "no good" because he liked to smoke weed and he couldn't have police around. Another had a boyfriend who was a doctor, but that didn't matter, he was dismissed as annoying. It didn't take much. Any excuse would do. Bit by bit, the people who had always been part of my life began to slip away. And I let it happen. I stopped calling. I stopped making plans. I didn't reach out or keep in touch. I isolated myself without even realizing it.

What I didn't see back then was how one-sided it all was because when it came to his friends and their girlfriends, I never found any faults. I just rolled with it. I adapted. I accepted. And in doing so, I lost pieces of myself I didn't even know were slipping away.

And then there was his dysfunctional family. A younger brother born from the wreckage his father allegedly left behind. An older brother who avoided the family entirely and, I was told, had once battled dependency. A sister who received no empathy during her own struggles. A niece who had a baby but little interest in raising her, leaving the responsibility to the great-grandmother. And his mother, always there, deeply entangled, often blurring the line between support and control. She wasn't malicious, but her constant involvement made it nearly impossible for him to grow into his own man.

I was the outsider in a story steeped in dysfunction. And still, I stayed. Until I couldn't unsee the truth.

Despite the silence, the shutdowns, the emotional distance, I still felt loved in small, consistent ways. One of them was how he always wanted me by his side, no matter where he was going. A quick run to the supermarket, a trip to Home Depot, errands that didn't require company, he'd ask me to come. It wasn't about needing help. It was about presence. It made me feel chosen, included. And those simple gestures were enough to keep me feeling secure, even when words were absent.

It was 2016, and life felt like it was sealed in a snow globe. He gave me a diamond necklace with a delicate little key. "It's the key to my heart," he said. And I believed him. And I wore it like it proved I finally belonged.

As Brazilians, we celebrate Christmas on the 24th. His American family celebrated on the 25th. It worked perfectly; we didn't have to choose. We blended and I felt welcomed. Like he was my safe place. And for a girl like me, safety had always been a luxury. But even in that supposed safety, there was a silence around the one person who mattered most, Vitor. He never tried to bond with him. Never showed interest. There was a coldness there I refused to name. I told myself it was just how he was. But now, I know better, love shows up, especially for the ones you love.

Then came Valentine's Day, 2017.

We planned a trip to Colorado, our first time snowboarding together. He introduced me to a couple he was close with, and we all went as a group. He paid for the stay and brought me chocolates. That trip marked the beginning of what would become our annual Valentine's tradition: a week snowboarding somewhere cold and beautiful.

With each passing year, I clung to that tradition like it was a symbol of our stability. Our growth. Our love. What I didn't realize at the time was that it would also be the first, and one of the last times he would pay for accommodations or transportation on our trips. After that and Hawaii, everything was split straight down the middle.

Our first anniversary was on June 10, 2017, at a trendy restaurant in Miami called Paris 6. He made the reservation, dressed up, and did everything right. But I had oysters. I didn't know I was allergic. The night ended with me sick, my stomach in knots, and what was supposed to be a celebration became just another memory cut short. But I didn't care. I clung to the idea that this was love.

We traveled often that year.

In 2017 alone, we went to the Bahamas multiple times, took a trip to New York, and enjoyed spontaneous getaways that felt like snapshots from a perfect romance. There was a carefree energy between us, like nothing could touch us.

For his birthday, I planned a surprise brunch with all his closest friends. He was beaming with joy and seeing him happy made me feel like I was doing something right.

By Christmas, we had a routine: Christmas Eve with my family, Christmas Day lunch with his mom, and dinner with his dad. On the surface, it looked like harmony, like we had built a balanced, blended life.

In 2018, the night before Valentine's Day, he called. I saw his name on my phone, but I didn't answer. I was tired. Disconnected. So, I went to sleep, unaware of what was happening outside.

What I didn't know was that he had parked by the gate and walked a life-sized teddy bear to my door, balloons in hand. The next morning, flowers showed up at my doorstep. He never brought it up. He didn't guilt me. He didn't complain. He just showed up with love, quiet, thoughtful, traditional. But looking back, his silence wasn't kindness. It was a pattern. He withheld, not just his voice, but his emotions. The kind of silence that leaves you wondering what you did wrong.

That year, I wanted to keep our tradition alive. On February 15th, I surprised him with a trip. I booked the hotel, bought the tickets, rented the car, made all the plans. Because in my eyes, love meant effort. And I was still holding onto the idea that we were building something real.

That was also the year we had our only breakup.

It lasted a week. Short, but loud.

I was uncomfortable with the way he ran things professionally. Some practices didn't sit right with me, ethically, emotionally. I voiced my concerns, he stood firm. I wanted ethics, transparency We fought. I left. He let me. But we got back together and over time, I began to convince myself, or maybe I just needed to believe it.

By our second anniversary, I had a business trip to San Francisco. He decided to tag along. We extended the trip to Los Angeles, then Hawaii. He told me we'd be staying at a friend's house in Hawaii, and I panicked. I wanted privacy. But he surprised me with a hotel. And on our anniversary night, he took me to a Michelin-starred restaurant with a custom-designed menu featuring our names. As I slept, he posted a heartfelt tribute on Facebook. He knew how to love in grand gestures. And I knew how to smile and say thank you.

But sometimes... it felt like he was performing. Like I was living in someone else's dream.

Then came the Maldives and Dubai. A dream trip for his birthday. I wanted it to be perfect. And mostly, it was. But even in paradise, we argued. I remember telling him, "You have a way of ruining my dreams." And I meant it. It wasn't the place; it was the energy. The shutdowns. The passive-aggressive tone. The silent punishments. He wasn't loud. He didn't hit. But he withdrew. And I mistook that for composure instead of control.

In 2019, we celebrated another anniversary, this time in Thailand. It felt like magic. Elephants, temples, turquoise waters. We looked happy. We acted happy. And I remember thinking, "This is what forever should feel like." I wanted to freeze time and hold onto that version of us.

That year, we did Halloween Horror Nights, took another one of my work trips to Rochester, extended it, and road-tripped through Canada, ending at Niagara Falls. More memories. More proof. More reassurance that I was with the right person.

But underneath it all, there was a quiet unraveling.

I clung to the trips, the matching outfits, the Instagram posts, the diamond gifts, as if they were shields protecting me from the truth: love isn't proven in five-star resorts or Michelin menus. It's proven in emotional safety. In presence. In real, unfiltered intimacy. I thought I had those things. But deep down, I knew we didn't.

There was emotional abuse. But I couldn't recognize it. Because I'd been conditioned to think abuse had to come with bruises. He wasn't yelling. He wasn't cheating. He wasn't vanishing. But he was twisting the truth, subtly, consistently, until I started doubting my own mind. It was gaslighting. And I didn't even know it yet. Creating a version of truth that only benefited him. And I, desperate to hold the fairytale together, became dependent on the illusion. I clung to his affection like oxygen, even when it became harder and harder to breathe.

That's what emotional abuse can look like. It doesn't always come with bruises. Sometimes it comes wrapped in diamond necklaces, anniversary menus, and photos of sunsets in the Maldives.

And then came 2020.

The world shut down. And for the first time, everything grew quiet enough for me to hear my own truth. The noise stopped. The illusions cracked. And I started to rise.

Chapter 10: The Year the World Shut Down, and I Rose

2020 started like any normal year. But just two months in, the world came to a screeching halt.

In early February, we took a quick trip to Las Vegas for a paintball tournament, full of laughs, adrenaline, gambling, and fun. We had big travel plans lined up for the year: Rome, Capri, Monte Carlo, Nice and Ibiza. It would have been a series of trips that felt like something out of a dream, a celebration of life and love in places I had always longed to see.

For the first time since our tradition began, our Valentine's trip, didn't happen. COVID-19 arrived like a thief in the night, robbing us of time, plans, and peace of mind. Travel was no longer an option, and even if it had been, the carefree joy that usually accompanied our trips was replaced with anxiety and distance. It felt strange to break the ritual, like something sacred had been paused. I tried to tell myself it was just the pandemic. But a quiet part of me wondered if this was the beginning of more things unraveling.

At the time, I was working as a Chief Scientific Officer at a local laboratory. When the pandemic hit, everything changed. My already demanding job became all-consuming. I worked more than 80 hours a week, sometimes sleeping at the lab. We were among the first laboratories in South Florida to provide COVID-19 testing. I was suddenly on the frontlines, doing news interviews, breaking down science into something people could understand, helping guide the public through fear with facts.

While most of the world locked down, I kept moving. I was labeled essential. I wore the badge of healthcare hero. But it didn't feel heroic, it felt like pure survival.

When the shortage of collection devices hit, I stepped in. I came up with the idea to mass-manufacture our own transport medium and validate alternate swabs. It changed everything. The National Guard visited our lab to learn the process I created so they could replicate it and assist the state.

In July, my CEO asked to speak with me privately and handed me a gift: a Rolex with a diamond dial. He had only given a watch like that to a handful of employees. I was surprised. I felt honored, proud, and grateful. And at the same time, profoundly exhausted.

With the maturity I have today, I realize that accepting a gift of that magnitude was a mistake on my part. The most professional thing would have been to accept it graciously and sell it, treating it as a bonus. But I kept it, and I believe that decision only helped fuel my boyfriend's paranoia and suspicion at the time.
He began to suspect I was having an affair with my boss. And from there, the seed of mistrust only grew. Small actions were suddenly met with skepticism, my daily routine became subject to subtle interrogation, and even my dedication to work was viewed with suspicion. What once felt like admiration turned into surveillance. And without realizing it, we stepped into a quiet territory, where jealousy disguised itself as care, and control wore the mask of concern.

Eight months passed in a blur of exhaustion, fear, and collective grief.
The days dragged on, heavy, as the death toll rose like a silent siren in the background of everything. Restrictions began to ease, but the world still felt stuck, and so did I. Then, in November, a friend went to get tested for COVID before a girls' trip to Colombia. She invited me. And without thinking, I said yes.

It wasn't just a trip. It was a reminder that joy still existed, that I wasn't entirely lost to the machine of survival. I needed something, anything, that could remind me I was still alive. That beneath the routine of pure survival, there was still room to feel, to laugh, to truly exist.

That trip was a lifeline, a brief return to the version of me that existed before the exhaustion took over. I rode horses freely through open fields, galloped like a wild woman, and laughed with my friends until my stomach hurt. It felt like I was breathing again. But the joy was short-lived.

When I came home, my family planned a Thanksgiving trip to New York. I abided by the state's restrictions and got tested. Turns out, I had already contracted COVID. I had to isolate, and I was terrified. I didn't know what the outcome would be. Thankfully, I survived, but I felt nearly every symptom.

Finally, in December, we decided to travel to Spain to celebrate New Year's, a trip I had been looking forward to for a long time, along with my family. But the new year arrived, 2021, and COVID didn't go away.
On New Year's Eve, December 31st, the laboratory I worked at was drowning with patient's specimens. While everyone else was celebrating, I had to board the first flight back and return to the frontlines.

My relationship began to quietly fall apart, I was working nonstop, and he spent his days locked inside the house. We were together but growing more and more distant.

It was during that time that I decided to chase a dream that had always felt just out of reach: I applied to become a Special Agent with the FBI.
When I was younger, I told my aunt I wanted to work for the FBI, and she laughed. "Stop dreaming that high," she said while my sweet grandma quickly rebated with "this girl can make nots out of a drip of water" That moment, those words, stayed with me.
So, when I got the official job offer, it didn't feel like I had just beaten the odds , it felt like I had proven something to every single

person who had ever doubted me.

Years later, I brought it up to my aunt, and she said she didn't even remember. But sadly, that's how it usually goes, the person who hurts forgets, and the one who feels... never does.

In the months that followed, I grew even closer to my boss and his wife. In March 2021, they got married at a private island resort, surrounded only by carefully chosen guests. The ceremony was beautiful. Peaceful. Powerful. And for some reason, it stirred something deep inside me, that long-forgotten dream of a little girl who once just wanted to get married.

When I told my boss I was planning to leave the company, he countered with a generous salary offer, one that I knew I wouldn't come close to earning even after years of working for the government.

At the same time, the FBI informed me that accepting the role meant signing a mobility agreement: they could relocate me at any time, to any place, without notice. Even personal decisions like marriage would require their approval.

And right there, standing between two completely different lives, I began to ask myself:

What is success, when your heart is still tangled in doubt?

Even though I had already decided to stay where I was, in the laboratory I help build, I continued with the process. I scheduled my polygraph.

Just a few days before the test, on April 1st, 2021, my boyfriend went out to dinner with a "friend." I called him, no answer. His phone was dead, as it often was, and I didn't think much of it. At the time, I truly believed our relationship was in a good place. I gave up calling, put my phone on Do Not Disturb, and went to sleep peacefully.

The next morning, I woke up to several missed calls, some from his parents, and one from a number I didn't recognize – when I called, I learned it was from jail. I was completely disoriented.

Apparently, he had dinner with a "friend," and after dinner, they went to a bar, Hijinks, where he later claimed he was possibly drugged. That "friend," by the way, was a man known for shady dealings and constant financial chaos, always surrounded by drama, always stirring something up, yet somehow still attached to our lives like a shadow I couldn't shake. The kind of person who always had a scheme going, always found himself in the middle of something shady, and yet somehow managed to stay tethered to our lives like a parasite we never invited in.

He told me he believed he had been drugged. And maybe that was true. He had a very expensive watch on him and said that out of nowhere, he became extremely aggressive, throwing chairs, yelling, behaving in ways that were completely out of character for him. So yes, he could have been drugged. But by who? A random person at the bar? Or the so-called "friend" who stood by and let him drive home in that state, never stopping him, never calling for help, never showing even a sliver of accountability?

He ended up crashing his car and was arrested on DUI and hit-and-run charges after trying to flee the scene on foot, running toward his house in a daze. At the end of the day, his father and I went to pick him up from jail, and when I saw the wreckage of the car, I knew, it was a miracle he survived. He told me he had hit his head hard and was in a lot of pain, but no one performed a CT scan or any kind of proper medical evaluation. Just a mugshot, a charge, and another layer of trauma sealed into the cracks of our already crumbling story.

And still… even after that night, after the chaos, the fear, and a brush with death, he stayed glued to that "friend", this "really good friend," as he used to call him. Not even that incident was enough to make him walk away.

Looking back now, especially after the timeline he later shared with me, and which I'll go into more deeply later, I wouldn't be surprised if that very friendship had played a significant role in intensifying all the behaviors that eventually spiraled out of control. It's as if he couldn't, or wouldn't, see the poison right in front of him.

Or maybe... a part of him had already chosen it.

I truly believe that may have been the moment everything changed. Something shifted after everything what unfolded in that bar , not just in our story, but in him. A psychiatrist even mentioned that, depending on where the blow to his head occurred, it could have caused permanent changes to his brain. That if something about him seemed different afterward, there was a real possibility he would never fully return to be the man I once knew.

Whatever the reason behind his actions, the consequences rippled straight through everything I had worked for.

The FBI special agent assigned to me didn't sugarcoat anything. He looked me straight in the eye and asked,
"How do you think the media would spin this? 'FBI agent's boyfriend is charged with DUI following a crash after leaving a bar.'"

That hit me like a brick wall.

Sometimes I still wonder if the erratic, self-destructive behavior that followed was a direct result of that evening. Maybe something truly changed in him. Maybe he lost his sense of right and wrong, his internal compass.
Or maybe... maybe that's just me, still trying to find logic in what was ultimately illogical. Still trying to excuse the inexcusable. Because that's what codependency does, it rewrites your reality. It convinces you that staying is strength, that loyalty is love, that sacrificing yourself is noble.

So, I stayed.
Not because it made sense. But because it felt familiar.
Because guilt speaks louder than clarity when you're used to carrying someone else's chaos.

I stayed at my job.

And as for my boss and his wife, the supposed source of his jealousy, he had never once expressed any discomfort or disapproval toward them. Not a word. In fact, after their wedding, we began spending even more time with them. He laughed, drank, smiled, joined dinners. There were no complaints. No tension. Nothing.
2021 was filled with adventures, Aruba, then Aspen for Valentine's Day with one of his friends and his girlfriend.

Then came Boca Bash.

Looking back, yes, I could have behaved differently.
But I was with my boyfriend. I was with friends. I was happy. Light. Free. I had asked him to bring the grill, some picanha, and cheese on a stick. When we docked beside my boss's boat, I asked him to start cooking, but somewhere between the music, the drinks, the dancing, and the laughter, I got swept up in the moment. I was having fun, enjoying myself, not watching the time or the dynamics.

My boss, very drunk, refused to eat unless I fed him personally. I laughed it off and fed him. No malice. No intention to disrespect. Just a chaotic party moment that, from the outside, looked worse than it felt.

And yes, if the roles had been reversed, I would've been furious. In the whirlwind of fun, I forgot the food. I forgot the optics.
But not the love. I still thought I was doing everything right.

At some point, someone told me my boyfriend was asking me to leave. I brushed it off, still caught in the noise, the fun, the distraction. When another guest came over, this time with more

urgency, I finally went to check.
He was livid. Fuming. Standing on the boat with a storm in his eyes. I stepped on board, and before I could say a single word, the ropes were already untied.
We were pulling away.
The silence on that ride back felt heavier than any shouting match. He didn't raise his voice, but his silence screamed but I continued having fun.

The next day, he confronted me. He didn't even know about the feeding moment with my boss, but he already felt disrespected. He told me I had treated him like the hired help. That I didn't even eat what he made. That I left him out.
It became a full-blown argument, the kind that leaves emotional bruises. And like always, I thought we had talked it out like adults. I thought it was behind us.
But with us... nothing ever really resolved.
The wounds never closed. They just scabbed over and festered in silence. He didn't know how to communicate his pain. He swallowed it, let it rot inside, let it turn into quiet resentment.

Still, we kept going, we traveled and this time, to my dream destination: Bora Bora. It was our fifth anniversary. Magical. Postcard perfect. The kind of trip that made it look like everything was fine.

My boss and his wife joined us. We flew on their private jet to Los Angeles, then flew commercial to Bora Bora. My boyfriend never once said a negative word. He smiled in photos. Toasted at dinners. Played the part. From the outside, we looked unbreakable.
But I had already started to notice cracks.

While we were still in paradise, I planned his birthday trip to Tulum, Mexico. I wanted to keep the momentum going. But that trip was the first time I saw something that shook me.
His ex, the one who had cheated on him, texted. I caught him smiling at his phone. When I asked, he told me who it was... but

then deleted the message before I could read it.
He had never done that before.
And in that moment, my stomach dropped. A red flag so loud it echoed through my body. Something had shifted.

A few months passed, and I found myself thinking more and more about the wedding we had witnessed on that private island. It had awakened something in me. A longing I had buried. So, I looked at him and said, "It's been five years. Either we take the leap, or I walk before the year ends."

In November, we attended a friend's wedding in Cancun. I had always dreamed of a destination wedding there, so I asked if we could visit a venue I had found, still under construction but offering a great deal. He agreed.
We weren't even engaged yet.
And still… Even without a ring, we signed the venue contract anyway, because deep down, I was clinging to a fantasy that felt safer than reality.

Then came my birthday.
I planned a big celebration at Dear, a local nightclub. I was barefoot, tipsy, glowing, completely myself. That version of me that only shows up when I feel safe, when I feel loved.
Little did I know, he had planned to propose. It happened right there in the middle of the party. And to be honest… I didn't even process it until I saw the ring.
Suddenly, I was engaged. And it felt surreal.

Later, we went to Vixens.
Had I known then what I know now, his vices, I would've never stepped foot in that place. But I didn't know. I was still high on happiness, floating in the illusion of forever.
We spent the night at the Hard Rock Hotel and made love like it was the first time. I was already planning a future I thought had finally begun.

But the cracks were widening.
He had deep, unresolved trauma around weddings, trauma rooted in his own family's chaos and emotional wounds. And me, pushing for commitment, for clarity, for something solid… it must've felt like pressure. Like control. Like a threat to his independence.
And because he had no tools to process any of that in a healthy way, that pressure became a fuse.
One I didn't know had already been lit.

And I was still too blind to see it.
Emotional abuse whispers that your pain is just the price of peace. And distorted perception wraps it all in a pretty bow and says, "This is what you always wanted."

I thought I had it all. I had the ring, the man, the career, the pictures. But deep down, I was already starting to disappear, fading into a version of myself built for someone else's comfort.

Chapter 11: The House, The Wedding, and The Undoing *(Part 1)*

Once I got engaged, I finally decided to move in with him. I had always told myself I wouldn't leave my parents' house to live with just a boyfriend, it had to be serious. It had to mean something. Engagement was that line for me.

I even tried to ease the pressure for him. I told him we didn't have to get legally married if he wasn't ready. That I didn't care about the paperwork. And if we did go through with it, I was open to a prenuptial agreement to protect his assets. I also mentioned I didn't want to change my last name, it felt like unnecessary work, and frankly, I didn't see the point.

Despite all my efforts to be flexible, he insisted we go all in. That we needed a real wedding. That I had to take his last name. "It has to be official, all the way," he said. On my birthday after we got engaged, he posted beautiful tributes celebrating me, ending one of them with the words "and my future wife."

He had a closet built for me and gave me a room, "my room." It was technically the guest room, but it became my space. My closet. My corner. I thought it was a sweet gesture. I thought it meant we were starting to build a home together. It felt like an invitation, but not a merger.

When I moved in, I assumed things would naturally shift, that his mom would understand there was now a woman in the house helping build this life with him. But that wasn't the case. She continued to come in unannounced, entering with the passcode, rearranging dishes, doing laundry, stepping into spaces that were no longer just his, but ours.

Don't get me wrong, she was kind, warm, and generous. A great mother-in-law. But there's a fine line between helping and invading someone's privacy, and that line was crossed regularly.

And him? He didn't take any action. True to his avoidant nature, he chose the path of least resistance.

Instead of having an honest conversation with her about boundaries, he told her she could come any time before 5 p.m., the hours I wasn't home. Did he really think that was a good idea? To frame it like I didn't want her there. That was never the case. I wasn't asking for distance; I was asking for respect. For formality. For the space to grow into that home as a partner, not as a guest.

But of course, he twisted the whole thing. As always, it was easier for him to deflect discomfort than to stand by my side.

But the change came fast. Almost too fast. As soon as I moved in, he started treating me like a roommate. The complaints were constant, about where I went, what I did, how I did it. Nothing was good enough. Nothing was easy. It felt like I had stepped into a relationship where the love had already expired, and no one bothered to tell me.

He came from a broken home. That much I knew. And while my own family wasn't perfect, it was picture-perfect on the outside, I had a solid upbringing. Both of my parents were present, together, and supportive to this day. But like I've said before, I carried a deep-rooted perception of rejection, which tainted even the good. Despite having love and structure, my distorted view made it feel like something was always missing.

He, on the other hand, carried real trauma. Deep scars from a life I wouldn't wish on anyone.

As I mentioned earlier, he had an older brother and sister from another father, who died by suicide. His mother eventually married his father and had him. He could've been the one to break the cycle. To rewrite the story. But he didn't. Instead, he clung to the worst parts of what he had witnessed.

Over time, he developed a deep hatred for his dad. And yet, in some twisted way, I believe repeating those same patterns, cheating, abandoning, manipulating, became his way of justifying it all. As if, by doing the same things, he could prove that his father "wasn't that bad." That dysfunction wasn't the problem, it was just life. He wanted to normalize what had hurt him, instead of rising above it.

His mom once told me stories, how she had to kick him out at sixteen, how he'd witnessed things no child should ever see: violent fights, physical abuse, police at the door. According to what was shared with me, his father allegedly had an affair with a prostitute. When she found out, she was done. No second chances. No reconciliation. She walked away. And instead of facing himself or taking any accountability, his father, perhaps out of spite or desperation, ended up marrying that same woman. They had a child together, but even today, in my opinion, it doesn't seem like there's any real love between them. Just cold tolerance. Most nights, there was wine, sometimes a bottle each. It was a pattern I couldn't unsee.

He claimed to hate everything about his father, his weakness, his behavior. But somehow, he still mirrored him. He mocked and humiliated him, even in front of others. He had to be right. Had to control the narrative. And if it wasn't done his way, it was the highway.

Let me be clear: some of these details were shared with me in conversations. While I trust the sources, I cannot confirm their accuracy, as I wasn't present and have no direct proof. These were not my lived experiences, they were shared accounts, recollections, and emotional retellings.

His mom, however, was different. She saw me. She understood me. She recognized the pain I was silently carrying and supported me in ways only another survivor could. She knew the weight of betrayal and the confusion it leaves behind, even though none of us, not even her, fully understood the extent of what was happening behind closed doors.

And while we haven't even gotten to the actual unraveling yet, I want to emphasize just how much her support meant to me. In a house full of distortion and dysfunction, she was one of the few steady hands reaching out to remind me that I wasn't crazy, that what I was feeling was real.

I was happy. I was hopeful. I was planning a future and a wedding.

A beautiful, three-day celebration set for our seventh anniversary, June 10, 2023. I sent save-the-dates. I poured over every detail. I built a dream.

That year began with our usual Valentine's Day snowboard tradition, but this time, it was a group experience. My boss and his wife, my fiancé, his best friend, and his girlfriend all came. We flew on my boss's private jet to Colorado and stayed in a stunning mountain cabin. A roaring fireplace, a private chef preparing our meals, a jacuzzi overlooking snow-covered trees, it was intimate, luxurious, fun. A celebration of love and friendship.

Then in June of our sixth year together, we took another unforgettable trip, this time to South Africa. I was beyond excited. I couldn't wait to experience the rawness of the jungle, to be immersed in nature. My fiancé, my boss and his wife, and I explored Cape Town, camped in Kruger National Park, then continued to the breathtaking beaches of Seychelles. We ended the trip with a short stop in Dubai.

In Dubai, he spent over $10,000 on clothes for himself. He bought me one pair of shoes. That was it. And no, I wasn't being materialistic. I was noticing. I was raised by a father who always put family first. A man who gave, who built a life with my mother based on shared dreams and joint effort.

With my fiancé, everything felt separate. His money was his. My money was mine. There was no union, no sense of building something together. It felt like I was trying to blend yin and yang into something harmonious, and he refused to blend with me. I was always kept outside, an observer in the life we were supposed to be sharing.

When we got back, a surprise letter was waiting. He told me the IRS had caught up to him.

He spiraled. Hired an attorney. Shut down emotionally.

Just a couple of weeks later, my boss's wife invited us on an incredible trip to Paris and Dublin, first class, fully covered, no accommodations needed. A literal dream come true.

But instead of sharing that excitement with me, he started acting like it was my fault. As if I had triggered the IRS situation. As if I had somehow brought chaos into his life.

His demeanor shifted, cold, resentful, withdrawn. And I didn't understand why. I had nothing to do with the taxes, the finances, or the decisions that led to that debt. But in his eyes, I became part of the blame.

He said no to the trip. He was "dealing with too much." And I understood, at least, I tried to. But he never explained the full extent of what was happening. At the time, I didn't even know the actual amount he owed, and truthfully, neither did he.

I told him, "If you're not going, I am." That had never been a problem before. But this time, it was. And I wouldn't realize just how much that shift meant until it was far too late.

His mother used to say: *"Opportunity makes the thief."* And I'd always respond with unwavering conviction: *"I trust him completely, I'd put both my hands in the fire for him."*
She'd calmly warn me, *"Be careful, or you're going to get burned."*

Trying to find a solution so he could come, I offered to help him make money by buying phones during release so he could resell them for profit, just like he had done every year. I ended up buying more than anyone. Still, no answer. No clarity. Just silence, right up until the very last minute when he confirmed he wasn't going.

He dropped me off at my boss's house, and I left.

Paris was fun. But one night, I drank too much and passed out. I didn't call him. The next morning, I apologized. I knew I should have. I wanted to be better. Another night, I tried to call him, and suddenly, it felt like he was ignoring me on purpose. Like he was punishing me for one missed check-in.

It was a dream trip for most people, but for me, it became the start of a nightmare

A month later, we flew to Cancun for our wedding planning trip. He was off, cold, detached, barely present. I understood that having both his mother and father in the same place might've made him anxious. But even knowing that, I still felt deeply alone.

It should've been the beginning of forever. It felt like the beginning of the end

From that point on, after the IRS situation, his answer to anything wedding-related was: *"We can't afford it."*
And yet, he spent over $10,000 on a tattoo, and another $5,000 on reptiles and cages.

The truth?
We had money.
He just didn't want to spend it on *us*.

Christmas passed. New Year's came. We went out to dinner in Miami to ring in 2023, our year. But New Year's dinner turned out to be a disaster. And I'm superstitious, so part of me blamed everything that followed on that night.

Still, our Valentine's tradition continued. This time, we went to Lake Tahoe, again flying on my boss's private jet with another couple. We stayed in a gorgeous lakefront home and genuinely had a good time. When we got back, he surprised me, he told me he was going on his friend's bachelor trip to Punta Cana.

I felt uneasy, but I agreed.

Then, one night, both his and the bachelor's phones were off. I spoke with my friend, the fiancée at the time. The stories didn't add up. I should've known then. But I didn't.

Then came my bachelorette trip, a luxury cruise, an incredible suite, chaos and tequila. I got banned from the cruise line for a year, if that gives you any idea of how wild it got. But I felt celebrated. Loved. My boss's wife and my sister planned every detail.

I had no idea what storm was brewing beneath the surface.

In March, we traveled to Brazil. He had business to take care of, and I needed to pick up one of my wedding dresses and get some cosmetic treatments done.

We started in Rio. It was fun, we had great moments with some of his clients who'd become close friends. Most importantly, we were there because my son wanted to attend the Coldplay concert. But even with the highlights, his behavior was off, borderline rude.

At his request, we booked two rooms so we could have privacy, since my son was old enough to enjoy his own space, but we weren't intimate at all. It felt like a waste of money and the tension lingered.

The second part of the trip was spent in my hometown, staying at my father's apartment. He seemed visibly uncomfortable, quiet, distracted, constantly looking for ways to leave.

While we were still in Brazil, one of my close friends had her entire wedding called off at the last minute. Everything had been paid for, everything planned, and the groom just walked away. I couldn't stop talking about it. I told him how devastating something like that would be for me. I asked him if he was still all in, if we were really doing this.

His answer was firm and confident:
"I'm not like that."
He looked me in the eyes, and I wanted to believe him.

Despite it being the weekend, with only one day left before our flight, he packed up and left early.

It felt like he couldn't handle being around my family, like he couldn't face them.
And maybe, just maybe, that was the real reason he left early. Maybe it wasn't discomfort, it was unspoken guilt. A weight he carried but wouldn't name.

At one point, he brought up that the IRS issue might be a problem. That perhaps we shouldn't go through with the legalities of the marriage. I was surprised, he had always insisted we go all in. But I didn't panic. We sat down, did our research, and found out that if we filed separately, it wouldn't be an issue.

Problem solved, at least that's what I believed.

Looking back now, I realize that conversation wasn't really about taxes. It was him planting the seed. Finding a loophole. Starting the gradual escape from something he no longer wanted.

I was focused on moving forward and he was already planning an exit.

In two separate moments, once in Rio and once again back home, I noticed something in his eyes. A distance. A vacancy. He looked like he wasn't even there.

Both times, I asked him:
"Do you still want to get married?"

The first time, he brushed it off.
The second time, he got angry. Defensive. Snapping at me for even

asking. He told me he hated that question. But how could I not ask? His actions were screaming what his words refused to admit.

And truthfully, sometimes, I even questioned whether *I* still wanted to get married. But I never said it out loud. I was too afraid that if I voiced it, it would become real.

I also questioned the lack of sex. I'm someone who craves connection, passion, that magnetic physical pull. So, it didn't sit right with me that I was always the one initiating. When I brought it up, he'd respond for a little while. But it never lasted.

I even joked, though I wasn't really joking,
"Seriously, I'm bending over in front of you in my underwear… throw me on the wall or something and do me."
He'd smile. But the fire wasn't there. That primal hunger… it was missing.

I was the fire in the relationship. I brought the heat. But a flame can't burn alone forever.

Then came May, just one month before the wedding. It was time for his bachelor trip.

I was already uneasy. The first one had left me unsettled. And now, the same gut feeling returned, stronger than ever. Something inside me just didn't sit right.

I remember walking into the reptile room with him, trying to keep things light, humming softly:

"You are my sunshine."
Then I looked at him and said,
"Please don't take my sunshine away."

He smiled and said,
"It's only four days. I'll be back before you know it. I won't take your sunshine away."

But deep down, I already knew.

My boss, who was also a groomsman, was supposed to go on the trip. They had planned to take the private jet. But at the last minute, my boss canceled, and the plans changed. They flew commercial instead.

Most people would've been annoyed. Upset. But not him. He was calm. Almost *too* calm.
And looking back now, I understand why.

When someone is focused on what they're *really* going for, the mode of transportation doesn't matter.
The destination does.

What came next destroyed me.

During his trip, my anxiety grew by the hour. I kept refreshing Instagram, hoping for any sign, a post, a story, anything that might bring peace of mind. But there was nothing. Radio silence.

Then I looked at his followers list and noticed a few random women I had never seen before.

It felt like a punch to the gut.

To the best of my understanding, he had been using steroids at the time. He'd spend four hours a day at the gym, obsessed with his physique. I hated it. I'd stay home waiting so we could have dinner together, only for him to come back late and casually say, *"I'm not hungry."*

I felt invisible. Like a ghost in the house, we were supposed to be building together.

Back to the trip, there was one girl in particular that stood out in his followers. I will refrain from mentioning her name here, for legal reasons. But something about her presence hit me like a red flag I could no longer ignore.

I picked up my phone and called him.

His phone was off.

My stomach dropped.

I texted his friend, the one he always talked down about but always kept close, and wrote,
"I know you're all disrespecting me."

Then suddenly, my fiancé called back on that same friend's phone.

I stared at the screen, livid. Boiling. But I didn't answer.

I was too angry. I knew that if I picked up, I'd explode. I'd ruin his trip.
So I made a choice:
I would wait.
We'd talk when he got back.

Before he left, he told me what time his return flight was. But the flight looked different, like it had changed. Naturally, I asked about it.

His response?
"For real? Why are you so insecure and untrusting of me? Why do you feel like I do things to deliberately piss you off? What have I done to make you act like this?"

Classic deflection. Master-level gaslighting.

And at the time, I still doubted myself. Still questioned if I was overreacting.
But spoiler: I wasn't.

Because what I would eventually uncover was brutal.

For anyone unfamiliar, gaslighting is a form of emotional manipulation that makes you question your own reality, instincts, even your sanity. When someone does something wrong and, instead of taking accountability, they twist the story until you're the one apologizing, for even noticing.

It's subtle. Insidious. Devastating.

He wasn't just avoiding the truth; he was reshaping it into a version that made me the villain.
Turning my gut instincts into weapons against myself.
That *I* was the unstable one.
That *I* needed fixing.

And I bought it. For far too long.

When he got back, we had dinner plans. As he walked through the door and saw the legal marriage documents on the table, his face changed. Panic, even if just for a second.

"What's that look?" I asked.

He brushed it off. *"No, everything's fine,"* he said.

But I didn't buy it. Not for a second.

Still, I let it go. For the moment.

Before we left, we sat down to talk, because something in me needed clarity. I brought up the girl he'd recently followed on Instagram. I wasn't trying to start a fight, but I was upset. His explanation?

"She works in the IV area of the gym's clinic. She's just a gym employee."

I stared at him, dumbfounded.
"So you went in for an IV... and somehow walked out with her Instagram? How is that remotely appropriate for a man who's about to get married?"

Then I brought up something that had been eating at me for years: there wasn't a single photo of me on his Instagram. Not one. In over six years.

"What kind of message do you think that sends?" I asked.
"To people who don't know us? To women you meet at the gym or the clinic?"

To me, it felt deliberate. Like he was making room. Keeping the door cracked open. Holding space to seem available, to keep his options alive.

In that moment, I felt like I didn't even exist.

We argued about that woman. I asked him directly if she was the real reason he spent four hours a day at the gym. As I scrolled through her Instagram, one of her stories had a message that hit too close to home, something about acting and proving desire. Whether or not it was about him, it felt like a dagger, it felt too pointed. Too coincidental.
It confirmed every anxious thought that had been swirling in my mind.

Still, we went to dinner anyway.

We sat down, ordered wine, tried to pretend things were normal. But they weren't.

Then he broke.

He looked at me and said the words that shattered everything:
"I don't know if I want to get married. I'm confused. It's all coming too fast."

My stomach dropped.

I couldn't eat. I turned pale. Cold. Numb.

Over 120 guests had already booked their flights and hotels to attend our wedding overseas. Friends and family from Brazil, Dubai, the U.S., all preparing to stand by our side for what was supposed to be the happiest day of our lives.

And here I was, sitting across from the man who had just lit a match to all of it.

One month. Just one month before the wedding.

The guests were booked. Dresses altered. Vendors paid.

And this man, the one I had given seven years of my life to, was unraveling it all in one sentence.

I spiraled. Quietly. Painfully.

That night, we went home in silence.

The next morning, I packed a small bag and left. I went to my cousin's house and told him I'd give him space to think, and that I needed space too. But it was unbearable. I couldn't sit still. My cousin and I drove all the way to Orlando and back trying to distract me. We even stopped at the casino in Coconut Creek, but my mind was still spinning. I was in complete chaos.

On the way to Orlando, I asked him directly if there was someone else.

He said no.

But later, over text, he admitted he had been having *inappropriate conversations* with other women. Just like that. As if it were casual. As if it didn't break me.

I asked,
"What kind of inappropriate conversations?"

He replied,

"I don't know… just harmless flirting. Telling girls we should go out, letting them know how to find me."

The kind of conversations a man about to get married simply shouldn't be having.

He later blamed it on the steroids. Said he was overconfident. Inflated. Disconnected from reality.

But the damage had already been done.

Eventually, after about a week, I returned home. We sat in the living room and talked. I was raw. Open. Desperate for clarity.

He was cold. Cocky. Distant.
Acting like a complete asshole.

He told me he didn't know what he was going to do. No empathy. No kindness. Just more pain.

So, I asked,
"If there wasn't a wedding planned, would we still be together?"

His answer?

"Probably not."

I was crushed in every possible way.

I started bargaining. Begging, really. I told him we didn't have to go through with the legal marriage, we could just have the symbolic ceremony and figure the rest out later. Just to survive the storm. Just to save face.

He agreed.

And then came the baby shower for one of his friends.

As the girls sat at one table, the guys stood off in the distance. I noticed my friend, growing upset. Saying her husband had been acting distant since his bachelor party, that something had changed. Meanwhile, I kept my eyes on the guys.

I've always been good at reading lips. Always.

At one point, I saw my fiancé pull out his phone, show the group something, maybe a photo, and say something along the lines of:

"F**, look at this. How am I supposed to get married?"

His friends smiled awkwardly. One of them said,
"Bro, you've got to figure that out."

My heart dropped, again.

Later, I was on the phone with my boss's wife, my best friend at the time, and I mentioned something that had just caught my eye: a sticker on his windshield that looked like a residential parking permit.

It wasn't ours.

What I saw felt suspicious. It led me to spiral, wondering what else I didn't know.

When we were ready to leave the baby shower, I confronted him. *"What's that sticker?"*

He claimed he didn't know.

Excuse my language, but how the f*** do you not know why a residential parking permit is on your car?

And what cut even deeper was what never came, he never brought it up again, never explained it, never tried to ease my spiraling thoughts. Just silence. The kind of silence that keeps you trapped in a loop of self-doubt and shame

I lost it. I screamed. I snapped. I told him I was calling off the wedding. That I was done with the rollercoaster. That I was shattered and exhausted and couldn't take another hit.

And that's when he said it:

"No. I'll go through with the commitment."

And so… I stayed.

I was unraveling faster than the wedding plans we'd so carefully assembled.
Because I didn't know how to walk away from something I had sacrificed everything to build.
Because I still believed love could fix it.
Because I thought commitment meant enduring pain in silence.
Because I wasn't ready to let go,
even though it had already let go of me.
I was still fighting for a future that only existed in my imagination.

Chapter 11: The House, The Wedding, and The Undoing *(Part 2)*

I stopped eating. The weight melted off. And still, I waited

I buried myself in the fantasy that it could still work. That love could still win. Even when every sign pointed to its death.

The wedding was perfect. A dream. And I want to remember it with joy, not hate. It was everything I had envisioned. Three full days, really, four unforgettable nights of magic.

But as much as I wish that were the end of the story… it wasn't.

Because as beautiful as it all was, I ended up marrying the wrong man.

We were supposed to fly to the wedding on my boss's private jet, but due to a financial dip at the laboratory, he couldn't afford the pilot or fuel. So, at the last minute, we switched to a commercial flight.

I didn't let it dull my spirit. I was bubbly. Excited. Living in the moment.

On the flight, I asked my fiancé to take a picture with me. Something simple. Just to capture the memory, even if we didn't post it.

He looked at me with disgust.

It sliced through my joy like a knife.

I still smiled. Still insisted we save that moment.

We flew out on Monday, even though the official events didn't start until Thursday.

That first night, we had dinner and drinks. I put on a beautiful lingerie set, wanting to reignite the spark. When I walked out, he was clearly taken aback.

I approached him, sat on his lap, and whispered:

"Let's enjoy this... because these might be the last few days you get to feel this chemistry, this fire."

He told me to stop saying that.

And just like that, we shared a week's worth of passion in a single night, and every night until Thursday.

Inside that room, it was fire and chemistry.
But outside... his behavior didn't change.

Cold. Detached. Distant.

One of his friends wanted to bring a Colombian prostitute as his date to the wedding, which I found incredibly strange. But since one of our guests had canceled last minute, I thought, *whatever.* What struck me as even more bizarre was when we were at the hotel, he suddenly pointed her out while she was on the carousel ride.

"That's her," he said.

I looked at him, confused. *"How do you even know that's her?"*

"I just do," he shrugged.

It was odd. Too specific. Too familiar. Something didn't sit right. Another red flag.

Then Thursday came. Guests started arriving.

And suddenly, he changed.

Warm. Friendly. Excited. Like flipping a switch. The shift was so sharp it was almost hard to believe.

That evening, we hosted a welcome meet-and-greet in the hotel lobby. It went beautifully. Some guests ended up going out to a club, and we almost joined, but stayed back at the hotel with the rest of the group. It felt like a night of peace. Of laughter. Almost like the dream was still real.

The next day was the beach welcome party.

Not to hype myself too much, but I looked like I had stepped straight out of a Beyoncé video. Confident. Radiant. Fierce. When he saw me, he was speechless.

But just before that, panic hit. We couldn't find the straps to my shoes. I started spiraling. He calmed me down, found an alternative pair, and we made it work.

Then came our pre-party photo shoot on the beach.

As the camera clicked, something strange happened, he kept apologizing. Softly. Repeatedly.

"Please accept my apology for what it is," he whispered.

I asked, *"For what?"* But he never gave a clear answer.

Just kept saying, *"Please, just accept it."*

And in that moment, I did.

I swallowed my questions. I tucked the unease away. I held onto what joy I could still salvage.

That night, the beach party began.

It was electric. Everything I'd dreamed of. Fire dancers, LED panels, fireworks, music vibrating through the sand, laughter swirling in the salty air.

It was supposed to be the highlight of the wedding week, and in many ways, it was.

I even played DJ for a bit, hyping up the crowd, soaking in the celebration. For a moment, everything felt perfect. Like maybe, just maybe, we could still pull this off.

And through it all, Vítor remained on the sidelines. He showed no interest in bonding with my son, never attempting to create a connection. His coldness toward the one person who mattered most to me was something I noticed… and tucked away.

But chaos always finds its way in.

My boss, admittedly very drunk, started play-wrestling with his daughter in the sand. It wasn't violent. Just tipsy silliness.

But it didn't sit well with my father-in-law. He puffed his chest, walked over, and decided it was his job to discipline a man he barely knew. Everything escalated from there.

Words were exchanged. Tensions flared. And suddenly, the energy shifted.

My fiancé was furious defending his father, enraged at my boss, and, indirectly, at me.

What was supposed to be a night of joy turned into confusion and confrontation.

I ended the night in tears.

I remember standing there, makeup smudged with salty streaks, completely lost. One minute I was dancing under fireworks. The next, I was a bride-to-be crying in the dark wondering why drama and pain had followed me even here, into what was supposed to be the happiest moment of my life.

Then came the ceremony.

We had taken private dance lessons to prepare for our first dance to *"Can You Feel the Love Tonight"* from *The Lion King*. But after he told me he wasn't sure he wanted to get married, we paused the lessons. It broke my heart. We only resumed once he agreed to "go through with it." But the magic had already been tainted.

The wedding day began with rain. Gloomy skies. I barely spoke. And when I did, my words were laced with anxiety and sharpness. My mind wouldn't stop spinning:

What if this man doesn't show up? What if he says no at the altar?

The rain wouldn't stop. And I started wondering if it was a sign.

My mom, deeply superstitious, quietly grabbed a bar of soap and threw it onto the ceiling. It's a Brazilian tradition, if you do that, the rain will stop. I clung to that superstition like a lifeline.

The hotel had made me sign a waiver confirming there was no backup plan. No indoor option. If it rained, it rained.

But 30 minutes before the ceremony, the sky opened.
The sun broke through.
A golden sunset painted the sky.
It was breathtaking.

I finished getting ready and walked down with my father. My mom, sister, brother, my son, the groomsmen, the bridesmaids, all made their way down the aisle.

Then it was my turn.

I walked in to *A Thousand Years*, smiling through the fear, locking eyes with the man I loved. The man standing at the altar.

And in that moment, all the fear disappeared.

The ceremony began. When it came time for the vows, I turned to the crowd and explained he wouldn't be saying any, but I would.

Then I read the most heartfelt words I had ever spoken aloud:

"My honey, my babe, meu amor, meu veizinho. You crossed my path in 2015, but it wasn't the right time for us. A year later in a boat, the universe gave us a new opportunity, and I knew I found my soulmate. Some may call it destiny, and I truly believe what is meant to be, will be. A relationship is never easy, and we learned that from the very beginning, the grass is never greener anywhere else. We have always chosen each other, and have worked on us, and I promise to continue doing that, day after day. Marriage can be a difficult path. Don't forget, I'm always your true north. I know I'm not the easiest, I'm stubborn at times, a bit of a brat, but you're assertive and patient. I promise to be less jealous, even when you have a sexy smirk. We complete each other with our perfect

imperfections. I choose you to do life with, hand in hand, side by side. I choose you to love with my whole being unconditionally. I choose you at the beginning and end of every day, and I would choose you in infinite lifetimes, in infinite worlds, in any version of reality. I'd find you in the middle of any crowd, and choose you, over and over. You make me proud every day, and I love you for who you are, for what you have become, and for what you will be. I love you for what we have built, and what we will build. I loved you once, I love you still, I always have, I always will. My forever."

People were in tears.

But inside, I was trembling.

I wasn't the glowing, bubbly bride everyone expected. I was scared. Like an animal backed into a corner. Waiting for the next blow.

After the ceremony, we took a few quick photos. But my gown was full and fluffy, and the heat and humidity were overwhelming.

Our guests were guided to the cocktail hour, something I had added to give the wedding that extra touch of magic. The golden sun dipped into the horizon. A saxophonist played trendy tunes, sparklers shot from his instrument. It was flawless. Picture perfect.

Meanwhile, I went up to the room to change into my second dress. Got my hair tied up, anything to feel a little more put-together.

I hadn't eaten all day. I was numb. Trying to hold myself together.

He came upstairs to change too, and once we were both ready, we were introduced as Mr. and Mrs. and walked into the ballroom together.

I was shaking. I sat down almost immediately, tried to eat something. Tried to ground myself. But I was still frozen.

Then the speeches started.

My brother and Samyra delivered the most beautiful, heartfelt words I've ever heard at a wedding. His best man and his dad spoke too, nice words, but nothing deeply personal or written with intention.

I cried during the speeches from *my* people.
And something inside me began to thaw.

The reception was breathtaking.

It was everything I dreamed of, down to the smallest detail: a light-up dance floor, flowers cascading from the ceiling like a glowing waterfall, a live band, the mirror man, the 360-video booth, a fun photo corner, a "sweets station" made just for him, and not one, but two wedding cakes to satisfy his sweet tooth.

It felt like I had stepped into a dream I never wanted to wake up from.

We had our first dance to *"Can You Feel the Love Tonight,"* the same song we had practiced to in our dance classes. Then I danced with my dad to *"My Girl."*

After that, the party kicked off, wild, full of energy, joyful.

But looking back, I realize something:
While I was laughing with my friends... he was off somewhere with his.
We weren't sharing the night the way most couples do. It wasn't bride and groom soaking in joy, it was two parallel realities. Close in distance. Worlds apart in spirit.

And to make things worse, he was clearly annoyed with my boss that night.

I understood why. My boss, who had always been kind and generous to us, started acting out. Drinking too much. Getting loud. His behavior shifted from fun to inappropriate, and it put me in an impossible position.

I was stuck between loyalty and embarrassment. Between keeping the peace and protecting my dignity.

Eventually, it escalated to the point where we had to ask security to escort him out.

It broke my heart.

This was supposed to be the happiest night of my life, and instead, I was managing chaos I never imagined I'd have to face.

After the reception ended, we had a penthouse booked for the after-party.

That's where I finally broke down.

I cried with a few close friends and told them everything, what had happened, how I felt like I had just run a marathon with no finish line in sight.

We drank too much. Fell asleep there. And the next morning, we did the infamous walk of shame, me still dressed like a bride, walking past the pool area at 10 a.m., heels in hand and heart still aching.

Then came Sunday, our farewell brunch and pool party.

I got ready and went down early to greet the guests.

He stayed behind, taking his time. Smoking weed, as usual.

That always came first.

The day was sunny and beautiful, but the air was heavy. Especially between my boss, his wife, and us. The tension from the night before still lingered.

They felt it. I felt it. Everyone did.

They sat at the opposite end of the pool, avoiding unnecessary confrontation.

Eventually, he came down and pulled me aside.

And that's when he gave me an ultimatum:

"When we get back, you're quitting your job, or there's no marriage."

I was mentally drained. Emotionally exhausted.
And at that point, I would've agreed to anything just to make it through the rest of the weekend without another explosion.

I wanted peace. I wanted to survive the wreckage.

But the chaos wasn't over.

Later that evening, I went looking for my son, who was 17 at the time, and found him sitting with my boss.

There were strange hand gestures exchanged, something off. I couldn't explain it, but my gut told me something wasn't right.

It looked like drugs were involved.

I lost it. I screamed at my boss. Sent my son straight to the room. Ended the night there.

Later, I learned it wasn't anything close to what I feared, they were just taking shots.

But that's how on edge I was. That's how fragile everything had become.

That night, something terrifying happened.

I was asleep when I suddenly jolted awake screaming. I thought he was choking me. He later told me he was just trying to stabilize me, to hold me down.

But in that moment, his face...
It wasn't his.
It was black. Blurred. Like a shadow version of him. The energy in the room felt dark. Sinister.

My scream echoed through the hotel; it was so loud that people across the resort heard it.

And then, just like that, I stopped screaming and went back to sleep.

As if nothing had happened.

I brushed it off. But deep down, I knew.

That wasn't normal.

That wasn't *nothing*.

Something spiritual happened that night.
Something unexplainable.
And I couldn't shake the feeling that I had just survived something I couldn't yet name.

When we got back, I did what he asked, I resigned.

That was emotional coercion at its finest, a subtle but undeniable pressure I felt I had no choice but to obey.

This wasn't just any job. It was a position where I made great money, where my closest friends worked, where I was respected and valued. What happened during the wedding week had been serious, yes, but deep down, I knew I should've handled it differently. I should've taken two or three months to transition, collected the bonus my boss had promised, and landed on my feet with a new opportunity lined up.

Instead, I folded under pressure.
I did what my husband demanded.

And now you might ask:

Did he help you financially while you were unemployed?

No.
Not once.

He gave me the money we received as wedding gifts, and that was it.

He didn't ask if it would cover my bills.
He didn't bother if I needed more.
His support ended at the surface.

Beyond that, I was on my own.

Still, I wanted clarity. I needed to know where we stood. So, I asked him directly:
"What are we doing?"

He looked at me, calm and confident, and said,
"We're married. We're doing this."

But the truth?

He meant *you're* doing this.

Because I was the only one showing up, and I walked away from that conversation feeling smaller than ever.

Then I found out I was pregnant.

Despite not wanting another child at the time, and despite having made the painful decision to terminate a pregnancy once before (his child), I had made a promise to myself and to God:

That I would never go through that again.

That I would carry whatever life was given to me, no matter what.

But I guess by divine protection, or divine intervention, it was ectopic.

I ended up in the ER. My fallopian tube had ruptured.

I could've died.

And he didn't even see how much damage he had done. Not just to me, but to the life we were supposed to be building together.

He barely stayed at the hospital.
He returned to work almost immediately, as if nothing had happened.

While I lay in bed, recovering from emergency surgery, trying to process the emotional and physical trauma, he didn't help.

No meals.
No comfort.
No checking in.
No care.

Just his usual excuse: *work*.
And *weed*.

If he had it his way, he'd work 24 hours a day, high and disconnected.
Completely detached from the reality of what I was going through.

He promised me we would get married, *really* married, on June 10, 2024. Our actual anniversary. He said we'd sign the papers. Make it official. Make it *right*.

He looked me in the eyes and gave me hope.

A false future.
Another illusion to hold onto.

But just like everything else, it was a lie.
Another manipulation dressed as love.

That date came and went. Nothing happened.

No documents. No vows. No commitment.

Just silence. Avoidance. Emotional abuse disguised as distance.

It was never about making things right.
It was about keeping me just close enough not to leave,
But far enough not to be held accountable.

That promise, like so many others, was never meant to be kept.

It was just another string in the web he spun to keep me entangled in the fantasy.

One weekend, we argued about traveling. I had simply asked if we were only going snowboarding and taking the one-year anniversary trip we had once talked about, or if we would take additional trips.

He snapped.

Accused me of only caring about trips. Said he wasn't spending any more money, as if he had actually paid for any of the trips I'd taken.

Later, while I was remotely connected to my computer for work, I overheard a conversation between him and his mom. He was bad-mouthing me. Complaining that I didn't want to sell some random purse for him and twisting it into a narrative that if something didn't benefit me, I wouldn't help.

The truth?
I didn't know where the purse came from. And I wanted to protect the integrity of my contacts.

But he kept going.

Said that if I thought getting married meant I was going to be "traveling around," I was dead wrong. That he didn't care what I thought.

I was livid. I confronted him.

Told him he was talking behind my back, painting a false image of me.

And like any skilled manipulator, he flipped it, accused me of invading his privacy. Said I shouldn't have been listening to a "private" conversation between him and his mother.

Wild, right?

I was robbed of a honeymoon.
Robbed of joy.
Every time I tried to plan something special, or asked for even the smallest gesture of celebration, I was met with indifference.

His business always came first.
I was always second.

It felt like I had married a ghost. Someone physically present, but emotionally vacant. A shadow of the man I thought I knew.

During those first months of our marriage, he made it clear: We weren't going out. Not to dinner. Not for drinks. Not anywhere.

He had suffered financial losses at the start of the year, and he declared that his entire focus was now on work.

And as much as he liked to call himself "the man of the house" because he paid his bills, the truth is, *I* was the backbone of the relationship.

I was the one booking the trips, making the reservations, renewing our passports, scheduling his doctor and dentist appointments, organizing our lives like his personal assistant, while still trying to be his partner.

I handled everything a grown man should've been doing for himself.

While I was out there being the alpha, handling life, he was hiding behind excuses.

And while I carried that weight like a warrior, the truth is…

I shouldn't have had to.

He should've been the one taking care of me.

I am a woman.
Delicate. Soft. Vulnerable.
I wasn't supposed to be the alpha in the relationship.

But I became her, because he left me no choice.

He was boring. Didn't like to go out. Said grabbing a glass of wine or a cocktail was "unnecessary." Traveling was always a burden, because in his eyes, it meant spending.

Fun was foreign to him.

And yet, I stayed.

I had so much patience. More than anyone should ever be expected to give.

I showed up for someone who never really showed up for me.

Then October came.

On the 24th, he told me he had to go to Colombia for a business trip. He described it as a mission to secure more clients and mentioned that his father would be going with him.

I was supportive. I stayed behind to care for the house and the dogs, not questioning much.

At one point during the trip, he FaceTimed me. His lips looked purple, like he'd been drinking wine. I asked about it. He casually said he had wine in his room.

It struck me as odd, he never wanted to have a glass at home. But I'd done similar things while traveling for work, so I let it go.

He returned on October 27th.

We spent Christmas that year the way we always had: Christmas Eve with my family, Christmas Day lunch at his mom's, and dinner at his dad's. But something felt different.

For the first time, I started to seriously wonder if something was wrong, financially.

He had always made it a point to give me nice gifts on my birthday and Christmas, the only two times of year that we exchanged presents. But that Christmas, he gave me sneakers and some workout clothes.

Don't get me wrong, I was grateful.

But it was a noticeable shift. Enough to make me pause.

I didn't say anything in the moment. But deep down, I started to worry.

Was something happening financially that I didn't know about? Was this just the beginning of a much bigger problem?

We spent New Year's Eve at his friend's house. Same crowd. Same routine. Same energy. It wasn't particularly memorable, just another night.

But it marked the beginning of yet another chapter.

And just like that, 2024 began.

No fireworks between us.
No special moment to carry into the new year.
Just the gradual continuation of a life I was starting to feel more and more disconnected from.

Even as I was still trying to hold it all together.

So, I turned inward. I started working out, focusing on my health, trying to find some sense of balance in this new chapter.

Valentine's Day 2024 was supposed to be special. Another snowboarding trip, just the two of us. Something I had looked forward to for months.

But he traveled sick. Really sick.

That first night and morning were brutal. I was up all-night taking care of him, worried, exhausted. In the morning, I drove through the snow alone to get medicine. Navigated icy roads just to make sure he felt better.

I didn't mind. I was happy to do it.
It was supposed to be our trip. Our time.

But then, he decided we were going to meet one of his friends at another mountain.

On the first run down the slope, they told me to take one path… and then they disappeared.

I waited at the bottom. Freezing. Furious.
Over 30 minutes passed. No one came.

Eventually, I called. After some frustration, we found each other again.

Despite everything, he sent me beautiful red roses to the hotel. And for a moment, that gesture softened me.

But just when I thought we might reconnect over a quiet, romantic dinner, he told me another couple had come into town, and he wanted to merge our dinner plans with them.

I agreed, trying to be understanding. But the restaurant had no space.

Another plan. Another moment… tainted.

February came, and it was time to celebrate my sister's birthday.

She had organized a party and invited many of our Brazilian friends, including some he didn't like.

Because of that, he flat-out refused to go.

I called him several times that day. Asking. Begging. Trying to convince him how much it would mean to me.

He never showed up.

I even told him none of the Brazilians he disliked were there. It didn't matter.

I was still alone.

During the party, I met a doctor, ironically, with the same first name as my husband. He was handsome, sure. But I didn't think much of it at the time.

I was just being myself, friendly, light, talkative. A social butterfly, as always.

The next day, my cousin called me:
"Who was that guy you were chatting with all night? The handsome one?"

I barely remembered. Until I saw him on Instagram.

Turns out, he worked in healthcare, specifically in the same specialty my lab had partnered with before. Naturally, we talked business for a bit.

That was it.

Nothing more.

Like I did with many others on Instagram, I followed him. Liked a few of his pictures. Nothing flirtatious. No ill intent.

Just casual, friendly interaction.

But as the year rolled on, the "business trips" didn't stop.

On March 4th, 2024, he announced he had to go back to Colombia. Another four-day trip. More "client meetings." More silence.

Again, I stayed home. Supported him. Took care of everything.

I didn't even ask to go, especially not to Medellín. I hadn't enjoyed it when I visited with friends, and honestly, I had no desire to return.

We were still in what he called a "no-spend" phase.

No dinners out. No entertainment. No unnecessary expenses.

And yet, during that same time, he thought it was perfectly reasonable to buy more reptiles, bringing the total to seven.

Between the cages, the care, and the animals, he had spent over $10,000.

He also completed another massive tattoo, around another $10,000.

It was *his* money, of course. He could do whatever he wanted with it.

But whenever *I* asked for something, something simple, like going out to dinner or planning a weekend away, I was "too much." I "wanted too much."

At one point, I even asked if he'd pay for me to get my lips done, just a small cosmetic procedure.

His answer was immediate and sharp:
"No. We're not spending any money."

Meanwhile, the wedding debt still lingered. And he made it very clear, he wasn't contributing toward it.

That responsibility, like everything else, fell squarely on me.

Then, in April, despite all the "no-spend" rules, he casually mentioned there was a guys' trip planned to the Dominican Republic.

My reaction was immediate:
"What? Again?"

They had already been twice. What could possibly justify a third trip?

I asked him directly:
"Is there a woman there?"

He called me insecure.

Said they just went because "everything's cheap", and then I may add, *even the women.*

That stuck with me. Like acid in my chest.

I told him I didn't want him to go. That I wasn't comfortable with it. That out of respect for his *wife*, he should stay.

It wasn't a controlling demand. It was a plea for basic consideration. For partnership. For loyalty.

He didn't argue. He just asked:
"Can you still watch the dogs?"

I said yes. Of course. The dogs were innocent. They had nothing to do with any of this.

But deep down, I knew.

It felt cruel.
He was free to travel. Free to disappear. Free to indulge.

And I stayed behind. Locked in the house.
Trying to make sense of why respect was always one-sided.

And so, he went.
April 18th. Another four-day trip.

While he was gone, I packed my things.

When he returned, we had a conversation.

He mocked me.

"You always say you'll leave, but you never do."

We agreed to give the relationship one more month.
I told him clearly:
"If I ever pack my things again, I'm gone."

He accepted it.

I asked him again:
"Were there girls on this trip? Is there someone else?"

His answer:
"No and no."

Obviously, I now know that was a lie.

Shortly after we became intimate again, I started feeling discomfort.

I went to my gynecologist.

On May 8th, I received my results.

I had tested positive for **Ureaplasma parvum**, a sexually transmitted infection.

I was shocked. Embarrassed. Confused.

Not once did I consider that he might have been unfaithful. That this infection didn't come from *me*.

I was prescribed two rounds of antibiotics for 30 days. The toll it took on my body was exhausting.

Still, I didn't tell him the truth. I told him it was just "an infection."

I was afraid.
Afraid that he'd twist it. Accuse me. Make me the villain in a story he was writing behind my back.

Later, in a rare moment of self-awareness, he said:

"I know it's not enough, but I owe you at least an apology, for my actions, for my family, for the past traumas and bullshit I brought into our relationship, and for not bringing things up sooner. I should've dealt with it head-on instead of resenting you for it."

And for the record:
Everything stated in this book is backed by physical proof.

June marked our first wedding anniversary, and our eighth year together.
June 10th.

We had plans to celebrate in Turks and Caicos, a trip I had been looking forward to for months.

But he got sick.

I drove him to the hospital, worried but calm, doing everything I could to stay grounded. I rearranged everything, flights, hotels, every detail, so we wouldn't lose the money we had spent.

He made it very clear: we weren't going.

He didn't want to travel while sick, understandably so. I truly *got* it.

But instead of gratitude, I was met with frustration.

He told me I didn't care enough. That I was only focused on the trip. That I wasn't being compassionate.

Meanwhile, I was juggling everything. His health. The hospital. The logistics. His moods.

Still, I was the villain.

There was no winning. No grace. Just guilt, layered over exhaustion.

Two weeks later, on June 22nd, we finally made it to Turks and Caicos for a five-day trip.

And on the surface, it was magical,
Snorkeling through crystal-clear waters.
Wakeboarding across turquoise waves.
Sunsets that looked like they were painted by God Himself.

But underneath it all… something was off.
I could feel it in my bones.

He kept wanting to go back to the hotel, said he needed Wi-Fi to "work." Locked himself in the bathroom for hours. Disappeared to smoke his weed, like it mattered more than the moment we were living in.

Everything felt like a drag. Like he wasn't really *there* with me.

Like I was just a background character in a story that no longer included me.

One night, we sat down for what should have been a romantic dinner, sunset behind us, the kind of moment you remember forever.

Instead, it turned into an argument.

He started criticizing one of his friends who had recently gotten divorced.

Then the conversation took a turn.
He started talking about how *women need to be submissive.*

Submissive. In 2024.

If you know me, you know I'm soft. Loving. I give the shirt off my back. I cook. I serve. I love hard.

But don't tell me I'm supposed to *submit* to you.
I do what I do out of love, not obligation.

I'm not your maid. I'm not beneath you.

I reminded him:
Yes, he paid the bills, but everything was *his*. I had no ownership in anything.

So no, in my eyes, he wasn't providing for *us*.
He was providing for *himself* and letting me exist inside it.

Even the trips, like I've said before, were always split down the middle.

Still, I stayed.

But things didn't change.

He refused to go out to dinner. Wouldn't grab a glass of wine at home. Didn't want to go anywhere or do anything.

He shut down.
And I started waking up.

I started focusing on *me*.

I found a therapist.
I wanted to feel like myself again.
Like the fun, happy woman I used to be.

I was tired of feeling like a caged bird.
Tired of walking on eggshells.
Tired of carrying the emotional weight for two people.

I didn't want to be his mother. His housekeeper. His emotional punching bag.

I was done picking up after him. Towels on the floor after one use. Clothes scattered everywhere. All the invisible labor of "love."

I didn't want to be the caretaker anymore.

I wanted to *breathe*.
To move.
To be my own woman again.

Not just for me, but for the life I was supposed to be building… whether with him, or without him.

One day, I was lying on the couch when he came over to lay on top of me and kiss me. I don't even remember what triggered it, but I called him a *"half-ass husband."*

He immediately pulled back and said,
"You're not getting a kiss, nothing," and brushed it off.

Later that night, he still came to bed. Still wrapped himself around me like a pretzel.
Still sent a sweet good morning text the next day.

But then, out of nowhere, he called me in the afternoon and scolded me for what I'd said.

He called me out for calling him a 'half-ass husband', but the truth is, that was the nicest way I could've said it. I was finally waking up.

I guess when the shoe fits… the sting runs deeper.

Chapter 12: When the Ground Cracked and Swallowed Me Whole

In August 2024, I noticed my husband slipping away. He looked defeated, drained of energy, bitter, and emotionally absent. After the promises and plans, this version of him was unrecognizable. He wasn't going out, wasn't eating well, wasn't even pretending to care. I found out he had lost a lot of money. And even though I was suffering in the relationship myself, my instinct was still to fix him. To show love where I wasn't getting any. That was the codependency talking, the distorted perception that if I gave more, maybe I'd be loved more.

As many trauma therapists explain, trying to fix someone is the core of codependency. It's the heartbreaking belief that you can save another person with your love. That if you just give enough, of your time, your energy, your heart, they'll finally be okay. They'll finally choose you. But love isn't supposed to be a rescue mission. And I was drowning while trying to pull him to shore.

So, I decided to plan a surprise birthday party.

I called his father to express my concerns. He agreed to host it at his house and said he would handle the food. I spent over $1,000 on decorations and sweets, trying to create something beautiful, something thoughtful. Something that would pull him out of the dark.

When I told my husband I needed him on Sunday for a surprise event, he didn't ask what it was. He just complained about what to wear, got dressed in silence, and sat next to me in the car without saying a word.

We pulled up to the house. Everyone shouted, "Surprise!" And for a moment, I saw it, shock, maybe even gratitude. But it disappeared fast.

He walked around, shook a few hands, gave shallow thanks, and then told the guests, "She told me we were going somewhere, and I didn't want to fight, so I came."

I couldn't believe what I was hearing. I was embarrassed and confused.

This wasn't just a dismissal. This was humiliation. In front of the very people, I had brought together to celebrate him, he made me look like I forced him to attend. Not a single post. Not a single photo together. Not a single acknowledgment that I had done all of that out of love.

That's what emotional abuse looks like sometimes. Quiet, sharp, and calculated. He turned my kindness into an inconvenience and made sure others saw it that way, too.

About a week later, I told him I had bought a new dress and wanted to go on a date with him. Just dinner, something to remind us of who we used to be, or at least who I hoped we still were. He looked at me and smiled slightly before saying: "Who's paying?"

It wasn't about the money. I could've paid for the meal ten times over. It was the tone. The way he said it. The coldness behind it. That was the moment I realized I didn't want this life. I didn't want this marriage.

By Wednesday, I told him I was moving out. I explained that I wasn't even getting the bare minimum anymore. I wasn't asking for luxury, I was asking for affection, for connection, for a damn ice cream on the Ave. And all I ever got was: "I can't spend money now."

So, I left, and while driving the truck away I asked God for a sign I was doing the right thing, and a miracle came in the radio. The song over the rainbow that was my late uncle's favorite started playing on Spotify, but this is a different version, it started with "Okay, this one is for Gabby". I get chills every time I remember.

As soon as I left, he pulled me back in, with promises of therapy, change, and accountability. But it was a script I'd come to know too well. Like many toxic patterns I now recognize, it was all performance. He went to therapy once or twice, refused to take medication, and thought that was enough.

We were still "talking," in that weird, gray area where I was emotionally available, and he was still emotionally cruel. He invited me to dinner one Friday and then canceled last minute because he was "exhausted." I still had access to the home security cameras we'd set up while living together. I saw him walk in at 5 a.m., with leftovers.

When I confronted him, he claimed he went to his friend's hotel to "hang out." I blew up. I told him I was done, that if I wasn't a priority, I didn't want to hear from him ever again.

After we separated, I did flirt briefly with the doctor I had met at my sister's birthday. It was harmless. Nothing ever happened. And still, I told my husband. I was honest. Because that's the kind of woman I am. I was separated and owed him nothing, yet I still chose to be transparent. That's the difference between him and I. And the saddest part of all of this is the way he was leading this relationship, one of us was bound to break eventually. He just got there first. But had I ever made that choice, I would've had the courage to own it. I would've sat him down, looked him in the eyes, and told him the truth. Had I made the bed, I would've laid in it, without lying, without deflecting, without minimizing. Because I know what accountability looks like. Because I don't hide. I don't manipulate. I don't destroy someone's reality with lies.

A week later, I noticed on the cameras that he went into the safe and took out a lot of cash. He didn't leave with his car. At 10 a.m., he returned home. I later found out that he had gone to a strip club.

I confronted him again. Like every coward, he responded with a web of lies.

First, he said he went to a strip club in Pompano. Then he said once it closed, he went to another one in Hallandale. I asked how he got home, and he said Uber. I asked for the receipt. He said his phone died and that a stripper ordered the Uber for him.

That was the most ridiculous part. He's paranoid about anyone knowing where he lives. He would never give a random woman access to his address.

I pressed harder.

Eventually, he admitted to getting lap dances.

I was furious. I told him I would go to the club myself and find out exactly what happened, every detail, every lie. That's when he suddenly added another piece to the story: after the strip club, he said, he went to Dandee Donuts with one of the strippers for breakfast.

Really? This man, who's rude, impatient, who can't sit still for five minutes, who's always in a rush to leave dinner, who hates waiting for anything, suddenly decided to sit down and have breakfast at 7 a.m. with a stripper? It didn't make sense. None of it made sense. And the more he talked, the more the puzzle pieces refused to fit. I knew he was lying.

One night at 3 a.m., after hours of going back and forth over text messages, he was responsive and engaged in the conversation, answering everything I asked. But the moment I said, "I'm coming over," he stopped replying. Silence. To me, that felt like avoidance, like he was trying to shut down the conversation before it could go any deeper. I couldn't let that happen.

So, I got in my car and drove to his house. I walked in like I always did, I knew the code and had lived there before, so I let myself in instinctively, still seeing that space as shared. In hindsight, I understand the boundary I crossed.

Yes, looking back, I know how dangerous that moment was. He sleeps with a gun next to him, and had he panicked just a second longer, he could have shot me. But I wasn't thinking about that in the moment. I just needed answers. As I opened the door, I screamed, "It's me, Gabby! I'm walking in, it's Gabby!" I said it loudly, clearly, hoping it would snap him out of sleep and avoid any confusion. Thankfully, it did. But the risk I took, the way I barged in hoping love would protect me, it's a terrifying example of just how clouded my judgment had become.

When I walked into the house that night, it was like stepping into a storm. He jolted awake, terrified, shaking, disoriented, thinking someone was breaking in. But it was just me. I had lived there. I had loved there. I wasn't breaking in, I was breaking down.

Amid all the yelling and chaos, it finally came out.
"Yes," he said, eyes dull, voice flat. "I had sex with the stripper."
I felt the floor collapse beneath me. It was disgusting.

It was vile. Violent in its simplicity. My heart shattered in an instant. And then, like any master manipulator, he tried to sew the pieces back together with poisoned thread. He pulled out the vows he never said at our wedding. Words I had longed for. Words I had waited for. But now they were soaked in betrayal. It was too late. And yet... part of me still wanted to hear them.

That's what emotional abusers do. As skilled manipulators, they know exactly how to confuse your heart and your mind. He knew I was hurting, vulnerable, desperate for something, anything, to hold onto. And so, he dangled love like a prize, trying to distract me from the betrayal I had just uncovered.

That's how emotional abuse works. It blurs the lines. It makes you question yourself. It paints moments of affection right after acts of harm, so you start to wonder, Maybe I'm overreacting. Maybe he does love me. Maybe I can forgive this. You begin to rationalize what should never be rationalized. You suppress the pain because they give you just enough hope to hold on. And before you know it, you're accepting the unacceptable, because your mind is no longer working to protect you. It's working to survive.

He began to read:

"My queen, I don't know how to tell you or express the love I have and hold in my heart for you. You have opened my eyes to many things, and I will forever be grateful for the pushes in life you have given me and will continue to give me.
We have gone through some of the darkest times and brightest times together, and I only pray that we come out on the other side together. Your beauty and intelligence have always kept me on my toes, and I am so glad I found my soulmate. Our compatibility is a match, and I'm sure no one would put up with me for as long as you have.
My babe has always been a trooper since day one, always sticking by my side, and I can't thank you enough for always deciding to fight for us.
These vows are coming months too late, and I regret not doing this the proper way, but I just want you to know… you mean the world to me.
I will always be there for you, and I will fight for us until the end of time. I'm your knight in shining armor, and you are my queen."

He looked at me like he expected me to melt. To forgive. To fall into his arms like the broken girl who once believed love could fix anything.
But I wasn't that girl anymore. I left at 6am to go to work.

I recorded it. Not because I wanted to remember. But because I didn't want to forget. I didn't want to be manipulated again. I needed the truth on record. Something to listen to when the gaslighting began again. Something to anchor me when my mind, trained by emotional abuse, tried to make excuses for him.

Because that's what emotional abuse does. It confuses you. It floods your brain with so many contradictions you begin to think the pain is love. It makes you rationalize betrayal. It coats manipulation in romance and hands it to you like a gift.

And just when I thought that was the bottom, when I thought nothing else could break me further, what came next?

What came next didn't just break me. It destroyed me.
And it became the moment I stopped recognizing myself completely. The moment I realized the version of me that loved him no longer existed.

Chapter 13: The Ruins Were Still Warm, and I Was Still Lying in Them

After he admitted to sleeping with the stripper, he tried to soothe the damage the only way he knew how, temporarily. He took me out to a romantic dinner at The Melting Pot. There were flowers waiting, and he picked me up like nothing had happened. I was still fragile, shaken to my core, but desperate to believe we could move forward. As we got in the car, I looked at him and asked, "That was it, right? That's everything? There's nothing else I need to uncover. Because I'm telling you… anything more will destroy me." He looked me in the eyes and said, "That's it. That's all." So, I nodded. I swallowed the pain. And we went out to dinner, pretending, for just a few hours, that we were still us.

When I left our home, I thought I was being strong. I told myself I was setting boundaries, standing up for myself. But the truth is, as a codependent person, it was just another desperate attempt to pull him closer. I wanted him to miss me, to realize what he was losing, to fight for me. And when I found out about the stripper, I spiraled, but somehow still tried to make sense of it. I told myself we were technically separated. That maybe it wasn't cheating. That maybe if I moved back home and we worked on our relationship together, we could rebuild. I bent the truth to protect my heart. I used denial like a shield because facing the betrayal head-on felt unbearable. That's what codependency does, it convinces you that pain is love, and that maybe if you just give more, they'll finally give you what you deserve.

A day after I moved back home, my phone rang. A private call. A woman's voice on the other end.

We will call her Kelly Lisa, she called me out of nowhere, her voice marked by a strong Colombian accent. "Your husband flew me to Santo Domingo for his bachelor trip," she told me. "There is proof. Sit tight, I will call you back with the reservation number."

I confronted him. I had called him as soon as I got the call, before I even had the flight information. I asked him about the name I had been given, and his response was textbook manipulation: "Calm down. Don't have a panic attack. Just leave work and meet me at home." He was 20 minutes away. I was 40. But I got there first. By the time he arrived, I could see he was scrambling, trying to get his lies in order. We sat down, and I asked again. That's when he said, flatly, "If she's telling the truth, you need proof." Then he got up, left, and resumed work.

As promised, she called again with the flight confirmation number. My stomach dropped. This wasn't a random mistake. This wasn't a lapse in judgment. This was a timeline. A plan. A parallel life he had carefully constructed behind my back. I called American Express myself. I handled all his travel documents, so I knew exactly what to ask. They confirmed the booking. The charge. So, I asked them to send the confirmation to both of us.

There was no more room for lies. The proof came. And when he couldn't lie anymore, he finally confessed: "Yes, I slept with her. It was my last hoorah."

I was so broken by then, so desperate to believe this could still work, that I told him I could forgive it. We had still gotten married. I wanted to save our story, if that was all.

Once again, I found myself trying to make the unjustifiable somehow justified. That's what codependency does, it makes you bend reality just to keep the fantasy alive. He said it was just that one time. And suddenly, everything started to make sense, the coldness before the wedding, the panic when he saw the marriage papers, the distant behavior. But in my mind, since it had happened before the ceremony, and since he still chose to go through with it, I convinced myself it could be forgiven. That love could still win.

That we could still make it. But it wasn't. And deep inside, I knew it.

That's when I remembered his email was still logged into my phone. He put it there himself for the camera access. Maybe he forgot, maybe he thought I was too naïve or maybe he thought he had broken me enough that I wouldn't look.

But I did.

And what I found… shattered everything.

This wasn't a fling. This wasn't one mistake. This was a second relationship. No, this was a second life.

Things were a complete mess, and my sense of trust was destroyed. Around that time, he mentioned he'd be going to a convention in Brazil, and the fear consumed me. I couldn't stop wondering if he'd bring her along, if they'd use that trip as another excuse to live out their fantasy. So, I did something I never imagined I'd do: I hired a private investigator in Brazil. I gave him his flight details, his phone number, and even a picture. I wanted to know if she was going too.

The night before his trip, I dropped off a letter for him, along with a rosary, still holding on to the hope that maybe, somehow, we could rebuild. The next morning, he called me. Sweet. Warm. Kind. And I panicked. I canceled the investigator. I was scared to lose him.

That's when the real nightmare began. The PI I had hired turned on me. He started blackmailing me, threatening to tell him everything if I didn't pay him an absurd amount of money. I told him not to worry, I would tell him myself. And I did. But for a full week, I lived in absolute terror. The PI had everything, his photo, his flight information, every detail. I was terrified something could happen to him.

Thankfully, he came back fine. But after that, he treated me like I was a criminal. I wasn't allowed in the house anymore. If we wanted to see each other, it had to be in public places. And just like that, I became the villain... for trying to protect myself from the truth.

During that same week, while he was in Brazil, I finally told him what I had discovered: that the "girl" from Colombia wasn't just some random fling, she was a prostitute. He called it absurd, and demanded I prove it. And I did. I had already found all her pages, her listings, everything. He couldn't deny it, and later confirmed he knew.

She was a prostitute. And I don't say that in a derogatory, jealous way, I say it in the most literal sense of the word. Her face, her body, her rates, her reviews, they were all publicly listed online, clear as day. Her services were publicly advertised, in her own words and images. This isn't speculation, it was self-published content. Photos, services, packages, even client feedback. She sold sex, attention, fantasy, even a girlfriend experience. And he bought it. Not once. Not accidentally. He knew exactly what she was, and he pursued her anyway.

Except this wasn't some sultry, irresistible temptation. This wasn't a passionate, forbidden affair like in some cliché movie. This was sad. Pathetic, even.

She called him her "teddy bear", or in Spanish, *Osito*, as if he were some sweet, warm, desirable man. But the truth? He wasn't soft. He wasn't charming. He wasn't tender. He was cold. Emotionally unavailable. Insecure. Rude. A man so detached from intimacy that he had to pay someone to pretend she wanted him. And she played the part perfectly, like they do. She knew exactly how to stroke his ego, feed him just enough fantasy to make him feel important, needed, worshipped. She gave him what I couldn't anymore, false adoration. Manufactured desire. Manipulated affection.

And he drank it in like it was salvation.

Because let's be honest, he wasn't a teddy bear. He was a walking midlife crisis in teddy bear cosplay. An emotionally stunted man-child cloaked in cologne, confusion, and entitlement. He wasn't some innocent soul who got swept up in something bigger than him. No. He chased this. He chose this. He paid for it, willingly, repeatedly, and without an ounce of remorse.

And the sickest part?

He loved it.

He loved being pursued, not for who he was, but for the illusion of power and importance he could buy. He loved the control it gave him, the validation it fed him, the fantasy it let him live in. Because in her world, this woman who sold desire by the hour, he didn't have to feel shame. He didn't have to face the emptiness of the life he created. He could pretend. Pretend he was admired. That he was special. That he was still desirable, still young, still in control.

But it wasn't love. It wasn't passion. It wasn't even lust.

It was a transaction. A soulless, rented illusion. A temporary escape wrapped in lies and laced with destruction. It cost him his dignity, his character, his humanity. And it cost me everything I had left, my trust, my sense of safety, the last pieces of my already shattered heart.

He didn't just betray me.

He discarded everything we had for a hollow, dollar-per-minute dopamine hit.

And I was the one left to clean up the wreckage. But even in ruins, something inside me was beginning to shift.

Chapter 14: A War I Never Asked For

She was a sex worker, a bottom feeder. And maybe that's exactly why he pursued her, because with someone like her, he didn't have to be better. He didn't have to try, evolve, or confront his inadequacy. With her, he could play the part of a powerful man. A false provider. A fantasy, in a country where the currency folds at the feet of the dollar, he became a king. A sugar daddy. He could throw around a few bucks and be worshiped, and she would play along, because that's what she did for a living.

With me, he had to face reality. I was strong. Independent. Successful. I had standards. I challenged him to rise, and he shrank. Instead of growing, he ran. He chose a woman who didn't love him, but who was paid to pretend. Because when a man can't rise beside a strong woman, he'll often retreat to someone who makes him feel bigger. Not better, just bigger.

He convinced himself I was having an affair with my boss, a man who was powerful, generous, and wildly successful. A man who built an empire and walked with ease. And beside him, I think my husband felt small. Insignificant. Like he couldn't compete. That insecurity turned into resentment. That resentment turned into blame. He needed something, someone, that would make him feel dominant again, powerful, desired. And he found that escort, who would give him all of that… for a price. Because when you don't feel like a man in your own home, sometimes you go looking for a stage where the script is written in your favor, even if the entire thing is fake.

I had asked my boss's wife to be my matron of honor, and I thought it made sense to include my boss as a groomsman too. He had agreed, showed no hesitation, no discomfort. But of course, that later changed. He became furious, claiming he never wanted him in the wedding party at all. That was his pattern, silent when decisions mattered, vocal only when it was too late. He never used his voice to participate, only to criticize. Rewriting history was easier than owning it

The affair started back in February, on that very first bachelor trip to Punta Cana with my friend's now ex-husband. That was the beginning of the end.

My then fiancé, was the one who asked for prostitution contacts. He pursued it. He wanted it. He got the number from someone loosely connected to my boss, but let's be clear: it wasn't the contact that destroyed everything. It was his choice. My ex-husband made the decision. He initiated the betrayal. He didn't just destroy our relationship, he shattered the sanctity of others, dragging innocent people into his filth. He entangled families who had no idea they were being pulled into the wreckage. And he did it willingly. This wasn't a mistake or a lapse in judgment. It was a conscious decision. A deliberate betrayal, executed with full awareness of the damage.

His actions played a direct role in the collapse of my friend's marriage. What he did, didn't just hurt me, it rippled through entire lives, tearing down trust, destroying love, and leaving devastation in its place.

In May, the time his bachelor trip rolled around, the one where I jokingly hummed "don't take my sunshine away", he already knew exactly what he was doing. There was no conflict. Only calculation.

He bought the escort tickets to meet him in the Dominican Republic, this time in Santo Domingo. This wasn't a typical bachelor party send-off. It wasn't some wild "last hoorah." It was the beginning of something calculated. With a woman he barely knew but likely thought would be easy to control, living in Colombia, far from the U.S.

And this same man, the one who came home unsure if he even wanted to get married because of "improper conversations", looked me in the eye and lied. I asked if there was someone else. He said no. But there was.

There was an escort who made him feel powerful, but only because she never challenged him. Because for a weak man, standing beside a strong woman doesn't inspire growth, it triggers insecurity. And instead of rising, he retreated. He chose ease over evolution.

I felt humiliated. All his friends saw me walk down the aisle to a man who was doing everything he could possibly do wrong behind my back. His friends watched, fully aware, while I naively believed in the love, I thought I had. One of his friends in particular, whose name I won't mention, again, for legal reasons, was, and still is, his pawn. A man he constantly belittled, criticized, and treated like trash, yet one who remained loyal to him like a trained dog. He gave him relationship advice as if he were some pillars of integrity, while simultaneously destroying his own. This so-called friend, the one who was always inside our house, always praising our relationship, always preaching about how much he wanted something just like what we had, this man wasn't my friend. He was his puppet. He did, and still does, whatever he is told by the man I was marrying. And the worst part? He knew. He knew what was going on. He knew the truth, and yet he chose silence. He chose loyalty to deceit over human decency. And what's even more infuriating is that my ex-husband constantly talked badly about him, mocked how lost he was, how directionless his life had become, and how he was now even considering moving to a different state because he couldn't seem to figure his life out. That's the kind of loyalty my husband inspired: one-sided, blind, and completely exploited.

Karma… oh, karma. It may take its time, but it never forgets. And it will bite every one of those who chose to cover his dirty business instead of doing the right thing.

And here's where life showed its cruel sense of humor, where the circle came full and sharp. Years ago, I broke up with Patrick in Punta Cana. And now, years later, the man I chose instead ended up sleeping with a Colombian prostitute… in Punta Cana. The same place where I walked away from something healthy, good, and kind. What a twisted, sarcastic way for life to remind me of my missteps. Of where I failed to choose right. It's almost poetic, except it's tragic.

He told her our wedding was fake. That it was all for show. That he wasn't really married. He fed her fantasy after fantasy, even the promise to help her get a visa, to bring her to the U.S., to build a future together. Meanwhile, I was at home, his real wife, clinging to a love that had already been sold off in pieces to a stranger.

Let's be real, if marriage was something he claimed to be so terrified of, then what kind of fantasy was he living with her? What was the endgame? Help her get a visa? For what, so she could eventually get deported? Because I would make sure of that. Or would he marry her? Would he risk all his assets, his business, his name, for a sex worker he barely knew but chose over the woman who stood by him through everything?

And knowing how he operates, from spite, not logic, perhaps after this book comes out, he might still do it. He might marry her. Just to show he's in control. Just to hurt me one last time. Because that's the thing about emotional abusers and narcissists: they don't feel guilt. They don't feel remorse. They don't process damage the way a human being should. They just crave control. And when they lose it, they self-destruct, and try to take you down with them.

There were receipts for everything. Rappi orders for late-night cravings. Random flower deliveries. Airline confirmations with her name spelled clearly, booked with the same care and urgency he never showed me, he never booked a single trip for us. Hotel reservations, each one a step deeper into his secret world. This wasn't a fling. It wasn't a moment of weakness. It was a parallel life, funded by betrayal and stitched together with lies.

In one of our arguments, he mentioned he FaceTime her family. Sat on camera smiling, charming them, probably while I was in the next room cooking dinner or folding his laundry. He pretended to be someone's boyfriend, someone's hope for the future, while wearing a wedding band. He looked them in the eyes through a screen and sold them a lie. And I'm sure they believed it, because that's what manipulators do best. They play the part flawlessly.

Most of his "business trips" weren't about business at all. They were calculated. Strategically arranged to avoid raising suspicion. He made sure to plan them around weekdays or keep them short so I wouldn't ask too many questions. But the first trip in October was different. That one was intentional. Her birthday fell on October 31st, and he knew staying away too long would trigger alarm bells for me, so he made it short and sweet. He returned home on a Friday, pretending it was just another business obligation. But what I didn't know then was that he had orchestrated the entire trip around her birthday. Once he was back home, he sent her 30 balloons to mark her age. Flowers. A teddy bear. He didn't just cheat, he celebrated her.

Then there was the guy's trip, the one he supposedly could barely afford to go on. My friend tried to protect me. She texted, saying our men's were going with one goal: to chase women. But I defended him. I told her I trusted him. I believed he'd never disrespect our relationship like that.

When he returned, I brought it up, not to accuse, just to be transparent. But he got defensive. Furious. Said she was making "serious accusations." He flipped the script, as he always did, and painted himself the victim. Suddenly, I was the problem. I was paranoid. I was the manipulator.

And remember Turks and Caicos? The constant bathroom breaks? The compulsive needs to be connected to Wi-Fi every second? The fights with me in the hospital while I was juggling everything, he was furious that I dared worry about a vacation. Later I learned why: he had secretly booked a trip for the same exact dates to go to her city, a plan he probably would've masked yet another "business obligation." That trip wasn't a coincidence. It was betrayal in disguise. He likely never even told her he was going to paradise with me. So, to keep the illusion alive, he had to act like he was working the entire time. He had to stay glued to his phone, responding to her messages, pretending he was somewhere else entirely. Every bathroom break, every moment on Wi-Fi, it wasn't random. It was a performance. One he chose to give while on vacation with the woman he was supposedly going to celebrate our one-year wedding anniversary.

But here's the thing, a relationship built on secrets is easy. It only survives in filtered snapshots and fleeting highs. There are no hard questions, no boring Mondays, no bills, no responsibilities. Just hotels, sex, lies, and fantasy.

When you're the other woman, the one kept in the shadows, you don't ask too many questions. You just take what you're given. Because in that role, you don't get the entire truth. You get whatever version of it fits the script.

Trips are easy. Adventures are exciting. When the backdrop is luxury and the days are filled with cocktails and sunsets, everyone seems wonderful. But the real test is in the ordinary, the day-to-day. The errands. The stress. The messy mornings. That's where character shows up. That's where love gets tested, and that's where most people fail. That's where we failed.

They stayed together on at least six different occasions; I have all the dates. Romantic distractions, nothing more. But what did they actually know about each other? Could they survive a Monday morning together? Did he know how she takes her coffee?

Because being fun on vacation is easy. Being stable, kind, supportive, and present when life isn't glamorous, that's the hard part. And he never showed up for that. Could she stand his routine?

Probably not. He's a difficult man. And believe it or not, I had a lot of patience.

Because what they had wasn't love. It wasn't real. It was performative. A story told in stolen time and stitched together with false promises.

Then there was the so-called convention in Colombia, one he had no real connection to. It was entirely planned by someone he worked with, but his greed, his obsession with what his coworkers were doing and how they were succeeding, drove him there. And of course, he couldn't go alone. He brought his side-kick escort along to "help," passing out flyers like she was part of the company. She was, after all, getting paid to do whatever he needed, right? I think he purchased the full girlfriend experience, and he just didn't realize how pitiful that truly was.

And the most revolting part? They involved a child. Her child. An innocent life caught in the crossfire of their web of lies. He played pretend daddy while ignoring the emotional wreckage he left behind in our home. That's not just betrayal. That's beyond reckless. That's evil wrapped in romance. And he didn't flinch. Not once.

He wasn't just cheating, he was investing. Building. He constructed a full emotional and logistical reality with another woman, using time, money, and energy that rightfully belonged to our marriage. To me.

And while I lay in bed beside a ghost, loving a man who no longer existed, he was fully alive in someone else's fantasy. Playing the hero, the provider. The man he had always pretended to be but never truly was. This wasn't just an affair. It wasn't a one-night mistake. It was a second life. A life I was never meant to find.

And me? I stayed home. Loyal. Loving. Feeding our dogs. Folding his laundry. Holding onto a future he was actively destroying behind my back.

He gave her the parts of himself I had begged for, without hesitation. While I had to fight for simple things like a dinner date or a movie night, she got teddy bears delivered to her doorstep. Flowers, gifts, attention. She got the version of him I had spent a year trying to pull out, and she didn't even have to ask.

The irony: He wanted to make it clear to me that she wasn't working anymore. That it wasn't transactional. And I looked him dead in the eyes and said, "Of course she's not working anymore. Because you're the one funding her."

Let's be realistic, any woman with a career like hers, who makes a living selling intimacy, doesn't just walk away from the business unless she's secured the bag. She didn't stop because she fell in love. She paused because her investment was paying off. He was paying for the fantasy. For the illusion of loyalty. For the privilege of being her one and only, at least until the money ran dry.

And he bought into it. Not just with his wallet, but with his heart, his lies, his time, and his soul.

He denied he was paying her, repeatedly, but I had already seen the truth. I had seen the receipts. The tracking numbers for gifts sent through DHL. Everything. I told him, "You're not paying for her body anymore, you're paying for her attention. You're buying validation. You're paying to feel wanted."

And she? She wasn't in love. She was clinging to the American dream. A visa. A way out. A passport through his pocket. She was calculating, playing her part well. And he loved it. He loved the illusion of being needed. Of being chased. Of being someone's fantasy. Even if it was all fake.

In one instance, when I learned about the affair I told him, calmly but firmly, "Pick up the phone and end it. Right now. In front of me."

I needed to see it. To hear it. To know that after everything, he was choosing me, the woman who had given him years, loyalty, forgiveness, and a future.

But he didn't reach for the phone.

He lowered his head and whispered, "I can't do that."

I stared at him, stunned.

He added, "Because I love you… but I also care about her."

And that… that's what set me off.

Because I had loved him without a price. Without pretense. Without an ulterior motive. I had carried his shame, his trauma, his family drama. I had sacrificed, forgiven, and rebuilt myself over and over just to stay by his side. I loved him in silence and in chaos, in success and in sickness. I loved him when he was unworthy of it, and I never once made him prove himself.

And now he stood in front of me, torn between me and a woman he met on a paid platform?

A woman he *paid* to pretend?

And somehow, I was the one being discarded. The one who had to beg for scraps of clarity. The one who was always "too much," while she was "just enough" because she came with no questions, no demands, just a price tag.

That moment wasn't just betrayal. It was erasure. It was watching everything I had built, everything I had endured, everything I had fought for… be reduced to a "maybe." The floor disappeared, and I will never forget the silence that followed. Because in that silence, I realized: I was no longer fighting for love.

I was fighting for dignity.

That's when I knew, I had to go to Colombia.

I couldn't sleep. I couldn't eat. I couldn't breathe without replaying what I had seen. The receipts. The flowers he sent her the day before our wedding and the flowers the day after the wedding. The random things he would send her. He was flirty. Romantic. He would sign his card with *TQM, Tu Osito, Te Quiero Mucho, Tu Osito*, which translates in English to *I love you, your teddy bear*.

While I, his wife, sat at home feeling invisible. Like a burden. Like a mistake.

So, I booked a ticket. No plan. No hotel. No one waiting for me. Just rage in my chest and truth in my bones. I woke up, showered, got a backpack and headed to the airport.

On the flight, I reached out to a friend. Someone who had walked through her own hell not long before me. Her now ex-husband had also made devastating choices, ones that shattered her world. And in a painful twist of fate, I would later come to learn that my own husband had played a role in the beginning of her downfall. A careless introduction. A reckless influence. One that triggered a chain of destruction in her life too.

Yet despite her own heartbreak, she extended me grace. She didn't hesitate to help. She connected me with someone she trusted in Cali, Colombia, someone who stood by my side through every moment. And that's the kind of strength only women who have survived betrayal can truly give each other.

She connected me with someone on the ground, a guardian angel of sorts, who met me at the airport and stayed by my side the entire time.

I wasn't reckless. I was deliberate. Strategic. I didn't want a scene. I didn't want chaos. I didn't go to destroy.

I went for the truth.

I asked the friend who was helping me to knock on her door. To tell her I was outside and wanted to speak. I was in her country, in a dangerous part of town, so I chose respect.

Not because I was scared, don't mistake that. I was calm. Controlled. Focused.

But make no mistake, I was not afraid.

She came outside with an air of arrogance, like she expected drama. Like she was ready for a performance.

But I didn't give her that satisfaction. I stood tall. I looked her in the eyes. And I told her I was there for clarity, not chaos.

That's when she started preaching. Started talking about "self-love."

Self-love?

From a woman who sells herself to married men?

From someone who builds fantasies with other women's husbands and calls it affection.

A prostitute, preaching self-love.

As if she even understood the term.

Let me tell you something: self-love isn't selling your soul for wire transfers and teddy bears. Self-love isn't tearing down another woman's home so you can live in a rented illusion. Self-love is healing your wounds, not weaponizing them.

She thought I was weak.

She thought I flew across countries to beg.

No.

I came to look her in the eye and make sure she knew:

The fantasy she was living in was built on stolen lies.

And the lies ended that day.

I didn't scream. I didn't cry. I didn't crumble.
I stood there, calm and collected, while she tried to defend the indefensible.

She wasn't a victim. She was a willing participant in the emotional assassination of another woman. And the worst part? She wore it like a crown.

She was low, crude, defensive, and filled with misplaced pride. Rude beyond belief, with an inflated ego that didn't match her reality. She looked and acted like a sex worker: tattoos across her neck, arms, chest, no class. Honestly, she wasn't even attractive, but somehow, she carried herself like she was God's gift to the world. She kept repeating the same line: *"My family is very dangerous,"* as if that was supposed to scare me into silence. As if I hadn't already walked through worse. As if flying across countries to confront the woman sleeping with my husband meant I could be frightened into submission.

She claimed she didn't care about money, excuse me?
The same man she was defending had been funding her lifestyle, paying her bills, sending her gifts, flowers, even teddy bears like a teenage fantasy. But according to her, she wasn't doing anything wrong. Because in her mind, our marriage wasn't "official." We didn't have kids. So, there was no guilt. No shame. Just entitlement. As if standing in front of her with our wedding album meant absolutely nothing.

And that's when my blood boiled.

Did she even consider that I had a son? A child who had grown up seeing this man as a stepfather figure? A boy who had already been through his share of pain and instability, and now would suffer again because of the choices these two adults made behind closed doors? Did she stop for even one second to think about the damage she was contributing to?
No.

Because to her, it was all about winning. It was about fantasy. About the American dream she thought she could buy with borrowed affection.

But I wasn't standing there to fight for scraps. I was standing there to expose the truth. And the more she spoke, the more I realized: she wasn't just a woman without shame. She was a woman without a soul. A bottom feeder trying to validate her actions by erasing the humanity of the people she hurt.

We spoke, but it wasn't a conversation. It was a one-sided, guarded exchange. He wasn't even there. It was just her. And from the moment she opened her mouth, it was clear she had no intention of being honest or decent. Every question I asked was met with deflection.
"I don't have to tell you anything," she said coldly.
"Your husband is the one who has to explain."
She kept her answers vague, smug, and condescending, as if I was the one invading her peace, when in reality, she had invaded my marriage.

She kept her phone angled toward me the entire time, clearly recording.
It wasn't about resolution or accountability.
It was a setup.
A performance designed to paint her as calm and composed, while I was the one on camera doing all the talking.

She rarely answered out loud. Instead, she would nod or shake her head, especially when I asked questions, she wanted to answer but didn't want him to hear later in the recording. She played it strategically, framing herself as the quiet victim while orchestrating the scene.

There was no remorse.
No empathy.
Not even a shred of decency.

She was callous.
Entitled.
Like she had every right to insert herself into someone else's life and marriage.

Like I was the problem for showing up with questions.

And still, I stood there.
Not to fight.
Not to scream.
But to face the woman who had helped destroy everything I built.

I said what I needed to say.
And when I saw there was no humanity left to appeal to,
I turned around and walked away, with more truth than I came with, and the unshakable knowing that neither of them deserved another minute of my pain.

I walked away that day with something she'll never have,
My dignity.
My truth.
And the strength to rise out of the ashes of what they tried to burn.

To him, I was always the liar: *"She never called you"*, he would say.
She claimed she never called me, and that was enough to erase everything I had to say.
In his eyes, she was innocent.
My words meant nothing next to her denial.

Not once did he stop to consider that maybe she had been angry. I moved out only to move back in so quickly. Did he ever consider that maybe her silence wasn't proof of innocence, but a reaction to betrayal.
That maybe he had sold her an illusion too?
He never questioned the narrative he built to protect himself, because in his world, I was always the one to blame.

As soon as I landed back in the U.S., I knew I had to act.
The rage. The betrayal. The danger.
It wasn't just emotional anymore.
It was personal.
It was protective.

I contacted the Colombian consulate and formally reported her.
I told them she had threatened me and expressed clear, malicious intent to move overseas, and potentially, my country.
I wasn't going to sit back and let someone who helped destroy my marriage manipulate her way into the U.S. under false pretenses.

I contacted every agency I could think of including federal agencies and immigration centers. I did it not out of revenge, but out of protection.
For myself.
For my family.
For other women like me.

She was not going to sneak her way into my country and continue the same game that ruined my life.

I gave full descriptions of her:
Her tattoos;
Her known aliases from adult websites;
The webpages;
Her social media;
Her intention to possibly enter with a tourist visa and overstay it.

And somewhere over the clouds, mid-flight, I opened my phone and emailed my now ex-husband.

No more gentle words.
No more pleading for love.
No more bargaining.

Just this: **"We are no longer friends. We are enemies. I'm coming for my things."**

By the time I landed, I checked the cameras.
And what did I see?

Him, dragging all my belongings into the garage. That's when I messaged him saying I was on the way and he better be there, or else I would have to involve the police.
Then I saw again, this time dumping my things outside like trash.

Like I was garbage.
Like I had never been his wife.
Never cooked his meals.
Never cared for our dogs.
Never loved him unconditionally.

That was his goodbye.
That was the respect he showed the woman who stood beside him through every storm.
That's how disposable I had become.

But not everything was outside.
Some of my personal belongings, intimate, important things, were still inside the house.

So, I called the police.

When they arrived, I explained everything.
Calmly. Firmly.

They were dismissive. Cold.

As if I was a stranger to my own life. One of them looked at me and said, "If he doesn't want you inside, you can't go in."

I pointed toward the door, toward my pictures, and said, *"I live here too. This is my house too."*

Eventually, they called him. He showed up. And the moment he did, I saw it in his face, guilt? Regret? No.

Just annoyance. Like I was a burden. Like I was still interrupting his perfect lie. Like he was inconvenienced by the consequences of his own destruction. But I was no longer the same woman he left behind. And he knew it.

I pointed toward the closet and calmly said, "I still have things in there."

He shrugged. "It's locked."

I looked down and saw the keys, right there on the nightstand. "There are the keys,"

I said, my voice steady. He picked them up, walked over, and opened the door himself.

The police officer stood in the hallway, watching. I turned to him and said, "It's okay. Everything's fine." I lied.

I protected him. Because if that officer had taken two steps forward, just two steps, he would've seen everything: the stash of weapons. The ammunition. Had the officer walked to the garage, there would have been more: weapons. Ammunition. Literal dynamite. I could've exposed it all. I could've ended everything for him right there. But I didn't. I simply gathered my belongings, packed up my dignity, and walked out the door.

What he didn't know was that I still had access to the cameras.

And I watched.

And I listened.

The moment I left, he picked up the phone and called her. **"My love"**, he said. With the same mouth that once called me *his queen*.

He laughed as he told her everything, how I came by, how I'd called the cops, how I couldn't even get inside. He mocked me.

Then he called his friends, bragging about how awesome it was that the police wouldn't let me in. He tried to justify his actions and paint himself as the victim, telling his friends I had been flirting with a doctor behind his back. Twisting the truth to fit his narrative.

But the reality was far from what he made it seem. I had told him about it myself, openly and honestly, and it happened during a time when we were separated. There was no betrayal. No deception. Just his desperate attempt to redirect attention from his own behavior by smearing my name. He needed a reason to excuse what he was doing. And instead of taking accountability, he chose to rewrite the story and make me the villain in a situation where I had been transparent all along. Like it was a game. Like I wasn't real. Like the woman who spent eight years loving him was just a punchline.

Then he called his family, and they came.

Not to help me, but to move the weapons and the explosives.

I texted him in fury: "I'm reporting you. IRS, authorities, whoever. I'm shutting you down."

His father told him, "Let her show her cards first."

Like I was the threat. Like I was dangerous. And then came the part that burned deepest. After they loaded the car with everything and the cameras kept rolling, I listened. They stood outside talking, joking, dissecting everything I had said, accusing me of lying because what I said didn't match what she had recorded. Yes. The escort. The one who recorded me in Colombia, nodding at certain things, staying silent on others, staging the perfect little show to make herself look like the victim. They believed her. They laughed at me.

And then... he said it:

"I should've just disappeared with her in Colombia."

Those words. I still hear them. I still have them, captured forever in the footage.

That was his truth.

Even after I had flown across continents, stood face to face with the woman who had destroyed my marriage, watched him call me a joke to his friends, seen my life dumped into the garage like disposable trash, I still wasn't free.

I went to my spiritual center. I needed answers. And what I learned shook me to my core. The choking. The darkness I felt after the wedding. It wasn't just a nightmare. According to my spiritual guide, dark spiritual work had been done against me, ritualistic and symbolic. They described voodoo dolls, something buried in a cemetery, and even an animal sacrifice.

To some, this may sound unbelievable. But I felt it. I lived it. And for those who understand spiritual warfare, you know exactly what I mean.

This wasn't just betrayal. This was war. A spiritual war.

When you're in the middle of a spiritual war, when everything around you feels heavy, dark, and unexplainable, you don't just encounter darkness. You also attract opportunists. People who see your desperation, your confusion, your hunger for answers, and they offer you quick fixes for a price. And when you're drowning, when you're terrified and desperate for relief, you pay. You don't question it. You don't stop to think. You just hope, hope that maybe this person can remove whatever curse, whatever energy, whatever unseen force is destroying your life. But most of the time, they can't. They don't. They just take advantage of your pain. And leave you feeling even more lost than before.

And still, two days later… **I apologized**. I apologized for calling the police. I apologized for threatening to shut him down.

Unbelievable, but I apologized. Because that's what emotional abuse does. It doesn't just hurt you; it reprograms you. It breaks your internal compass so thoroughly that you start mistaking cruelty for love. You start believing that you are the one to blame for your own devastation.

It whispers lies until they sound like truth:

"You're too dramatic."

"You're too emotional."

"You're overreacting."

It teaches you that your pain is a burden. That your boundaries are attacks. That your voice is dangerous.

So, you silence it. You shrink. You surrender. It rewires your brain to feel guilt for demanding respect. To feel shame for having needs. To feel like you are the villain for daring to react to the chaos someone else created. And that's what codependency does. It doesn't look like weakness; it looks like sacrifice. It feels like love, but it's actually survival. You tether your worth to their approval. You convince yourself that if you can just be better, quieter, more forgiving, they'll come back. They'll choose you. They'll change.

Even after everything, after the cheating, after the manipulation, after the voodoo, the lies and the humiliation a part of me still hoped he would wake up one day and say: "It's you. It's always been you." But that part of me wasn't love. That was the part he broke. A piece of me still hoped he'd wake up and choose me. Because that's how far I had lost myself. That's how deeply I had been trained to betray my own instincts in order to protect his lies.

Looking back now, the red flags weren't subtle, they were screaming. But when you love someone with a codependent heart, you learn how to silence the alarms.

You convince yourself that loyalty means blindness. That love means endurance. That doubt is disloyal.

He started taking long, frequent bathroom breaks, disappearing for fifteen, twenty minutes at a time, phone in hand like it was an extension of his body. The phone was always facedown. Always locked. Always off-limits. He guarded it like it held the crown jewels. And maybe it did, because it certainly holds the truth. He stopped coming to bed with me.

We used to fall asleep wrapped in each other. Our breath synced. Our bodies tangled. But toward the end, I'd wake up alone. He'd be on the couch on his phone, or I wouldn't even know what time he had crept in. The bed got colder. And so did he. His absence became louder than any argument we ever had.

Even the small things became betrayal. The vaping, for example, it seemed harmless. But even that was done in secret. I'd catch the scent sometimes. And when I'd ask, he'd deflect, minimize, gaslight. So, I swallowed those doubts. One by one. Like poison pills coated in denial. Because that's what happens when you live with emotional abuse. You don't just ignore the truth. You learn how to bury it inside yourself, and smile through the ache.

Each little red flag felt like a paper cut. Not big enough to scream over, but deep enough to bleed. And I let them pile up until I was covered in invisible wounds. Tiny stings that eventually formed a full-body ache I couldn't name. And still, I smiled through it. Because I didn't know I could ask for more.

The truth is, **I didn't love him anymore**.

But I still needed to win. I needed to be enough. Just once in my life. Because my entire life, I believed I was rejected. From childhood to motherhood. From friends to lovers. And this man, this liar, this manipulator, this man who dumped my clothes outside like garbage, he wasn't just a heartbreak. He was the living proof of every fear I had ever carried, every wound I thought I had buried.

He was proof. Proof that I was never the one. Never the final choice. Just a warm-up. A placeholder. A convenience.

And so, I kept fighting. Not for the relationship, but for **the illusion that I mattered**. That I was lovable. That I was worth choosing. That someone, somewhere, would finally pick me and mean it. That's the twisted thing about emotional abuse, it doesn't just break you. **It reprograms you**. It convinces you the breaking was your fault. That maybe if you were quieter, sexier, less emotional and more understanding than he wouldn't have done what he did.

Codependency is a sickness.

It rewrites the script in your head until betrayal sounds like an accident, and humiliation feels like compromise. I knew he was lying. I knew he was gaslighting me. I knew. But I still sat across from him, hoping for the tiniest breadcrumb of remorse.

I still answered the phone. I still reread the old messages. I still fantasized about a version of him that never really existed, one I had stitched together from broken promises and fake apologies.

That's what **distorted perception does**.

It takes a man who destroyed you and paints him as the victim. It makes you the villain in your own story. And because I was so used to rejection, so used to fighting to prove I was worth keeping, I believed I had to work harder. Love deeper. Bleed longer.

Even when I found the emails. Even when I smelled the alcohol on his breath and heard the lies in his voice. Even when I stood in front of another woman's house, wedding album in hand, heart in pieces, I still didn't believe I deserved better.

That's how far gone I was.

That's how tightly the trauma had wrapped itself around my soul. It wasn't just a relationship.

It was an addiction. To hope. To validation. To the fantasy that if I just endured a little longer, the ending might change. But fairytales don't grow from emotional abuse. And love doesn't bloom in places built on lies. I didn't lose him. I lost the illusion. I wasn't stupid. I was in survival mode. And survival makes you do things that don't make sense.

It makes you love the hands that strangle you.

It makes you call the monster "babe."

It makes you believe that if you just prove yourself one more time, they'll finally see you. But he never saw me.

Because he never wanted to. He wanted someone to worship him, not someone to challenge him. And the more I shrank to fit inside his broken world, the more I disappeared from my own.

That's not love. That's destruction. And I almost didn't survive it. He liked the power. That much was clear. With her, he could feel like a king, someone important. But let's be honest: he was never going to marry her. He was never going to risk his assets, his money, or take on the responsibility of bringing her and her family to the United States. Especially not with a child in the picture.

That would mean real commitment.

Real consequences.

And for a man like him, fantasy was always better than reality. He liked the illusion of being wanted without having to show up for anyone. He liked the feeling of control, not the weight of responsibility. And rationally speaking? It's laughable. So naïve. So painfully gullible. Of course, she "quit." Of course she was "available." That was the entire point. She knew exactly what she was doing. You don't walk away from money until the next check is guaranteed.

He thought she was special. She was strategic. That's what she did for a living, she made men like him feel like gods so she could secure her next move. The list of gestures he did for her still makes me sick. He sent her an iPhone. A Christmas iPad for her son. On Valentine's Day? She got flowers too, just like I did. Random, expensive gestures.

And "tu osito"? To me, it was never sweet or romantic. The way she used it felt infantilizing. He wasn't cute or cuddly. He was secretive. Manipulative. A man with the emotional maturity of a teenager. Maybe that's why it worked. Maybe being called a teddy bear by someone he was financially supporting made him feel adored. A man living out a fantasy. In her world, he was "tu osito", and that gave him power.

Now for the final twist? This wasn't even an original story. It was the exact same story his parents lived. He didn't break the cycle, he copied it. Word for word. Same ethnicity. Same city. Same pattern of betrayal. Same emotional blueprint. He didn't evolve. He inherited destruction. And repeated it. At the expense of a woman who loved him. At the expense of a future that could have been beautiful.

But I broke the cycle for myself. I didn't stay in that legacy. I walked away from it. And with every step I took, I returned to myself. I came back stronger, clearer, wiser, and finally free. Or I thought so…

Chapter 15: Even the Silence Was Loud

I wish I could say I never spoke to him again.
That I burned the bridge, blocked the number, and never looked back.
But *healing isn't linear*. And trauma doesn't end with a climax, it echoes.

After everything he had done, after all I had uncovered, after Colombia, after the bouquet message that still rang in my head, TQM, tu osito, after watching him call another woman "my love" on the cameras in the home I helped build…
I still let him back in.

Because that's what emotional abuse does.
It carves a home inside your brain and convinces you it's shelter.

I went to Brazil; he still watched all my stories. Still liked my pictures. Still hovered like a ghost who wasn't ready to be buried. And I let him. Not because I loved him, but because I hadn't learned how to unlove the version of myself who still needed his approval.

I wanted him to see what he lost.
I wanted him to regret it.
But more than anything, I wanted to stop feeling like a discarded thing.

When I came back from Brazil from my cousin's wedding, he asked what I was doing for Thanksgiving. I told him I'd be alone. He said, "I will not allow you to spend this holiday alone, can I bring you dinner?"
And I said yes.

Why? Because part of me still believed maybe he had changed. That maybe now he understood the damage. That maybe the version of him I knew could somehow return.

But he never returned. That man was a mask. A costume worn just long enough to bait the hook.

He brought the food, said a few kind words, and left like a ghost leaving a meal at a grave.

Then I left for Singapore and Bali, it was my 40th birthday and I went on that trip with Samyra. And once again, he crept in. He offered to drive me to the airport. I said yes again. I thought I was being strong, calm, indifferent, above it all.

But codependency wears a thousand masks. It pretends to be healing when it's just another way of staying attached. He followed my trip on social media like he was part of it. Liked everything. Sent comments. Pretended we were still connected. And I let him. Because pretending I was still wanted felt better than facing the truth.

When I landed in Bali, he called. Said he missed me. Said he wished he was there. Said everything except the one thing that mattered. So, I asked: "Have you cut ties with her?" He paused. Then said: "No." And in that moment, I broke again. But not like before. This time, I didn't break down, I broke free. I told him: "Then don't ever contact me again." And I meant it. There was no more bargaining. No more asking him to choose. No more begging for decency.

I had been humiliated, lied to, emotionally beaten down to the bone. And still I had offered him my presence. My softness. My access. But all he had ever given me was uncertainty. Disrespect. Betrayal. That's the reality of distorted perception. You think "he's not that bad," because you survived it. You think "maybe I overreacted," because he cried once. You think "maybe I'm just hard to love," because he said so. But no. I wasn't hard to love. I was hard to manipulate when I stood in my truth. And he didn't want love. He wanted power. He wanted to be able to destroy me and still be invited to dinner. To lie to my face and still have access to my body. To split himself between me and a prostitute and still get praised for honesty. That's not healing. That's delusion. And I was done. For real this time. But that wasn't the end. Because life doesn't always give us clean exits, and pain doesn't always come with a warning.

When I got back from my trip, it was my birthday. He invited me over to see the dogs. And when I arrived, he had roses and a balloon. One balloon. It wasn't a celebration. It was a breadcrumb. A hollow gesture that looked like effort but felt like guilt.

And then I did something I swore I wouldn't do, I sat down with him. I talked.

I asked the question that had been clawing at my mind: "Are you two dating? Like, boyfriend and girlfriend?"

He wouldn't even say yes. He just said, "We know our roles."

What the hell does that even mean?

It means nothing. It means everything. It means she was playing her part, and he was playing his. A private performance of dysfunction masked as mutual benefit.

But even then, he was so embarrassed by it all, he wouldn't admit it to his friends. To them, he kept saying he just wanted to be alone. He was lying to everyone, not just me. Even the people closest to him didn't know the full extent of the double life he was leading.

Such a sociopath.

Still, I was in the thick of it. Still poisoned by the illusion that if he didn't admit it to them, maybe he still wanted me. Maybe this wasn't over.

I told him, point blank, that if he was going to cheat, he might as well cheat on her with me.

Because that's how far I had fallen. That's how distorted my sense of self had become. I didn't even care about being chosen anymore. I just didn't want to be last. I didn't want to be discarded. I didn't want to feel like the fool.

I wanted to be the return to sender. The one he came back to. The proof that no matter how far he wandered, he always circled back to me.

And then came Christmas.

I walked into his house in a tiny dress. No underwear. I sat on the counter like it was mine and told him to pull his pants down and do me.

He did.

He asked, "What are you doing?"

I said nothing.

Because it didn't need explanation. That moment wasn't about him. It was about me. About releasing the rage. About burning the illusion to the ground.

But… We moved to the couch because he's not tall enough to reach me on the counter.

The sex wasn't passionate, it was reclaiming. It was desperate and dark and powerful in its own twisted way. I wanted to take back what was mine, even if I didn't want him anymore. I wanted to stain the memory of her with my presence.

I wanted to humiliate her without ever saying her name.

All because he couldn't keep it in his pants. All because he needed to feel wanted. All because he wanted to play out some twisted fantasy while destroying the woman who loved him.

He gambled with my health like it was nothing.

Chapter 16: The Illusion of Peace

You would think that after everything, after the cheating, the lies, the betrayal, the STD, the humiliation, I'd be done.

But I wasn't.

Because when you've been conditioned by emotional abuse, when your mind has been rewired by trauma, when you've been groomed into believing love means endurance, "done" doesn't come so easily.

I told him not to contact me. I meant it. But inside, a storm was still brewing. I kept checking if he was watching my stories. Kept wondering if he would text. Kept hoping, not for him to return, but for him to finally realize what he lost. I wanted closure. I wanted recognition. I wanted revenge.

That's the distorted perception trauma leaves behind. It makes you think you need validation from the same person who invalidated you every step of the way. I didn't want him back, I just wanted him to feel the void he created. To sit with the loss. To regret me.

But abusers rarely mourn what they destroy. They just move on to the next thing that makes them feel powerful.

He had no intention of being accountable. He knew exactly what he was doing. Every lie was calculated. Every omission was deliberate. Every fake apology was part of the manipulation.

And yet, I still fantasized about the apology that would never come. The honest conversation. The accountability. The tears.

That's what codependency does, it keeps you chained to hope even after reality has burned the bridge.

I thought I was healing. I started meditating, writing, traveling. I told myself I was done. But deep down, I still wanted the fairytale ending, where he shows up, confesses everything, and begs me to take him back.

Why? Because then I'd finally feel worthy. I'd finally feel like I mattered. I'd finally win.

That's the curse of never being chosen as a child. It turns you into an adult who needs to be chosen by the most unavailable person in the room.

I kept going back to the same emotional slot machine, hoping that this time it would pay out. But all it gave me was silence. Emptiness. And the echoes of a woman who used to be me.

My worth was never supposed to be decided by a man like him. A man who told everyone he was "alone" while living a full-blown relationship with a woman he was ashamed to claim. A man who gave me an STD and flowers in the same breath. A man who couldn't even say he was dating her because he knew how pathetic it sounded out loud.

He didn't just lie to me, he lied to his friends, his family, himself. He lived in a world of image and illusion, terrified of accountability.

And yet, I kept mourning the version of him I imagined. The man I thought I married. The man I believed in. That man never existed. He was a character. A mask. A bait.

And I took the hook.

This chapter of my life wasn't about romance. It wasn't about love. It was about waking up to the truth: I had been living in a house built on manipulation, and I kept trying to make it a home.

I was trying to heal while sleeping in the ruins.

I didn't just lose a relationship; I lost my sense of reality.

The truth is, when you've been emotionally abused, the breakup doesn't end when the person walks out. It ends when the delusion dies. And mine took its time.

I'd be having a good day, and suddenly I'd remember something he said, something small, something I didn't question back then, and it would hit me. That wasn't love. That was control. That was manipulation wrapped in affection. That was a crumb, dressed up like a feast.

I started replaying moments like a crime scene. The vacations, the fights, the gaslighting. I remembered him accusing me of being "too emotional" when I asked for more, or insecure when I accused him of doing something wrong (when in fact, he was). I remembered how he made me feel crazy for having boundaries. How every conversation somehow ended with me apologizing for needing anything at all.

That's what made it so hard to leave. Because the pain didn't always come with violence. It came with confusion. With questions. With blame. With "you're too much" and "I just need space" and "you're overthinking things."

And the worst part? I believed him.

I believed I was asking for too much. I believed I had issues. I believed I had to shrink myself to keep the peace. I lost my voice trying to keep a man who never truly listened.

But slowly, the fog started to lift.

I realized he never loved me the way I loved him. Because love doesn't lie. Love doesn't humiliate. Love doesn't ask you to prove your worth every damn day.

He didn't break me because I was weak. He broke me because I was strong, and that scared him. I was the mirror he didn't want to face. The one who saw through his charm, his stories, his carefully curated identity.

So, he did what manipulators do. He made me doubt myself. He made me second-guess my instincts. He made me feel like the problem.

But I wasn't the problem. I was the consequence. I was the reckoning. I was the reminder that he couldn't hide forever.

And still, the codependent part of me mourned the dream. Still wanted to believe that somewhere deep down, he cared. Still searched for signs of remorse in the way he lingered on my page, or commented on a post, or watched my stories like a stranger begging to be let back in.

I had to teach myself that someone watching your life doesn't mean they want to be in it. Sometimes they just want to make sure you're not doing better without them.

Not always. Not consistently. But enough.

Enough to start sleeping through the night again.
Enough to stop checking his Instagram.
Enough to stop blaming myself for what he chose to destroy.

That's when I started to reclaim pieces of myself.

Not all at once. But piece by piece.

The way I dressed. The way I laughed. The way I walked into a room without flinching.

He tried to erase me. But I remembered. And now I was rebuilding.

And this time, the foundation wasn't made of manipulation. It was made of truth.

Even when it hurt.

Chapter 17: The Chains of Codependency

I didn't even know what codependency was. I couldn't name it, couldn't define it, couldn't recognize it in the mirror. But I was drowning in it.

It wasn't until I broke that I finally started to learn what it was.

It began with a book, Codependent No More by Melody Beattie. I devoured it like my life depended on it. Because, in many ways, it did.

That book taught me how to detach without hating. How to surrender without losing. How to let go without giving up. It said that when we finally release the need to control, the thing we've been desperately hoping for might actually show up, like a miracle. Sometimes it doesn't. Sometimes it never does. But either way, you still win. Because when you let go of trying to fix someone else, you finally have a chance to fix yourself.

You don't have to stop loving someone to detach from them. You don't have to become cold, or mean, or numb. You just must stop setting yourself on fire to keep someone else warm. You can still care. You can still be soft. But you don't have to tolerate abuse. You don't have to carry someone else's pain and pretend it's yours to fix.

I didn't know what cognitive distortions were. I didn't know what boundaries really meant. I didn't understand why I kept bargaining with someone who made me feel worthless. All I knew was that I couldn't live without him.

That was the thought I had over and over again:

"I'm not happy with him... but I can't survive without him."

It's not just romantic. Codependency can happen in families too, between parents and children, siblings, friends. You can be codependent with your son. Your family can be codependent on your patterns. But until you see it, until you name it, you are enslaved by it.

My healing didn't begin in comfort. It began in complete emotional ruin.

Then came **January 1st, 2025.**

The new year began with me deciding we were getting back together. I had made up my mind.

He had texted me not long before saying, "Anything you ever need, I will always be here. I'll do anything for you."

So, I took him at his word. I went to his house. I told him that it wasn't a want, it was a need. A desperate, aching, hollow need to be with him.

He looked confused. Hesitant. He said he didn't know what to think, given everything that had happened between us.

That same month, I started seeing a new therapist. She was recommended by one of my best friends, Samyra. In the beginning, it was three, sometimes four sessions a week. I was fragile, crumbled. Just trying to survive.

At that point, I was still cycling through the stages of grief: denial, bargaining, anger, depression. I couldn't even think about acceptance yet. I wasn't ready to let go.

A week into everything, I took the weekend for myself. I needed to check out, to truly disconnect, in order to check in with myself. That meant no distractions, no noise, and most importantly, no phone. I needed silence, solitude, and space to breathe. When I finally turned it back on that Monday, I saw the messages. He had been concerned. He said he was so worried he had been on the verge of calling my family. And for a brief moment, I felt like maybe he still cared. But then I remembered, worry isn't the same as love. And silence doesn't mean absence; sometimes it's the only way to hear yourself think.

But we did it anyway. We agreed to start over, secretly. Just between us. No social media. No friends involved. Just us trying to "work it out" in private.

That was the first sign. Because secrecy is never the foundation of something healthy. It's the first layer of control.

I deactivated my Instagram. I stopped talking to people about us. I buried my truth so he wouldn't feel "exposed." I told myself this was part of rebuilding, part of healing. But it was just more of the same abuse, wrapped in a new package.

If I wanted to be with him, I had to follow his rules.

If I wanted peace, I had to stay silent.

If I wanted love, I had to swallow the betrayal and pretend it didn't happen.

My feelings didn't matter. My needs weren't considered. Everything revolved around his comfort.

I started walking on eggshells again.

I was terrified of saying the wrong thing, asking the wrong question, bringing up the wrong memory. I was terrified to ask if he had really ended things with the prostitute. Terrified to push him away. Terrified of being alone again.

Then came Valentine's Day.

I was panicking. I didn't know if I was going to be the only woman receiving affection that night, or if the sex worker was still in the picture. My chest felt like it was caving in.

He invited me over for dinner. I got dressed up, did my makeup, wore something nice. I had no idea if we were going out or staying in, because remember, we were "secretly together."

When I got there, he had cooked a nice meal. It was quiet. A little awkward. He handed me pink roses. He had never given me pink roses before. For eight years, I always got red.

It hit me wrong.

Later, I asked him, gently, "Was there a reason you didn't choose red roses this time?"

He brushed it off. "I just wanted to try something different."

But something in me knew. Red roses meant love. Passion. Commitment. Pink was safe. Distant. A diluted version of affection. Just enough to say I care, but not I love you.

I started to feel like I was being breadcrumbed. Fed just enough affection to keep me quiet, but never enough to feel secure.

Throughout February, we stayed in this secret arrangement. He went hunting a couple times. I stayed home with our dogs. There weren't any rules for him, but there were always unspoken rules for me.

In April, I tried to win him over again. I bought us UFC tickets. Something I knew he loved. I told him over a month in advance to save the date for a surprise, and of course, he decided to go hunting that week.

He got back just a couple hours before the event. We went, but he was tired. Exhausted. Whatever intimacy or connection I had planned for that night vanished. He couldn't be bothered. I swallowed the disappointment, again.

Then came May.

One day, I was deleting old screenshots from my phone, screenshots of his e-mail I had taken back then. And I found one, a hotel reservation I had seen before during the chaos of losing my ground. But this time, I realized something chilling: I had misread the date by the year.

It wasn't innocent. It wasn't business. It was a reservation for a local hotel in Pompano, near one of the places I come to learn he is addicted to: Strip Clubs.

I got to his house before him that day. I still had the freedom to come and go. We were, "fine", or so I thought.

When he arrived, I told him I wanted to show him something and I didn't want him to dance around the answer, then showed him the screenshot.

"Do you recognize this hotel?" I asked.

His face gave everything away, I already knew he had done something bad.

But he said, *"Nope. Don't recognize it, never been to it."*

I looked him dead in the eyes and said, *"Interesting. Because this came from your email."*

He immediately turned cold, and said I needed to get out of his e-mail. I am not sure why, but this man thinks I am some type of hacker that can bypass any verification settings to get to his e-mail. He told me he didn't feel comfortable and said I needed to leave. I asked him why? Why was I being told to leave for asking a question?

He said I didn't have to leave, and I genuinely understood I didn't have to leave at all. Then he told me he was going to his dad's house. I said ok, and I walked into the bathroom to shower. Surprisingly when I came out, he looked at me like I had done something wrong.

"What are you doing?" he asked.

"I thought you were going to your dad's; I didn't know you wanted me to go, I thought I was staying."

"No", he said, *"I told you I want you to go home."*

I broke down crying. Panicked. I begged, again. *"Please, if I go home, it's going to raise red flags with my parents. Let me stay."*

He let me stay. But everything was cold. Distant. Awkward.

I couldn't get out of bed that weekend. I was so depressed and I stayed until Sunday night, then went home.

After that, he completely avoided me like I was a disease. By this point, I was already spiraling; panic attacks, PTSD flashbacks, and a growing dependency on Xanax to calm me down. But it only made things worse. The relief was short-lived, and as soon as the medication wore off, I was right back in the same state of terror. The panic would return stronger, fueling a vicious cycle of taking more pills just to feel okay, just to sleep my life away.

The next day, he texted me and asked how I was doing. I told him the truth: horrible.

I was confused after everything that had happened over the weekend, and I didn't even know if we were still together. Then he called, and at that point I tried to get some clarity, but all he said was that we couldn't be together right now, and that I wasn't the problem. It was him. His guilt. His shame. I didn't know what to do anymore. I was unraveling. I had lost myself, and I was struggling to cope or accept what was happening. All I could do was beg, because that's where I was: broken, desperate, and still trying to hold on to something that was already gone.

I started crying on the phone. I told him I didn't know how to live without him. That I had no purpose. That I was afraid of what I might do and told him my suicidal ideation was growing because I could not see life without him. I told him I would check myself in the clinic because I didn't know what I would do to myself.

He then *asked me to not* go to the clinic. He suggested we could do couples therapy and told me it would be beneficial so that all cards are on the table and that we would be able to heal together to move forward. He also went as far as suggesting he would start his own therapy, just like I did mine. That I should just hold on and give time and everything would be ok.

So, I did. I told him I had my private therapy coming up on the following day and I would contact my therapist and see how this would unfold.

I immediately contacted her, and she was reluctant. She didn't think it was a good idea because now she would no longer be my therapist, she would be ours, and the dynamic would change. But I insisted. I told her I was sure it was the right course of action and suggested we try one session. If she felt it wasn't appropriate, we could stop. She agreed, and before proceeding, she drafted very specific rules to be followed.

In the first session, he cried endlessly. He spoke about regret. About guilt. About how he felt robbed of the chance to chase me down because I had never let him fight for me. He said that if we were going to move forward, it would take both of us, individually and together. He even brought up the hotel picture and admitted that he realized the truth was going to catch up to him, and that he wasn't doing anything he could be proud of.

He sounded convincing. Emotional. Almost… sincere.

But something didn't sit right with me.

And over time in those sessions, the truth started to surface, little by little, piece by piece, like a horror film unraveling in slow motion. And the more I learned, the more I realized that this man, this man I had loved for almost a decade, was never who I thought he was, slowly he was showing his true colors, and they were dark and ugly.

In those sessions, and through texts I still have saved on my phone, he admitted to more than I thought I could ever handle.

Let's start with the hotel incident I mentioned previously. I had misread the date by the year, but when I looked again, it turned out to be the exact weekend I was in Paris, the same one when I called him, and he didn't pick up. In earlier chapters, I said it felt like he was giving me payback for my one missed check-in. But the truth was worse than I thought.

He said he booked it for a girl he had met when he went to do a money exchange, I assume some Brazilian girl. Not a prostitute, just a regular woman. He invited her out to dinner, fully intending to sleep with her afterward. This was during our engagement, but in his small mind he said he had to do it to see how comfortable he would be and if he really loved me.

Just like a narcissistic sociopath, he admitted that during dinner, he kept thinking about me *"where is my babe"*, *"what am I doing"* and that he wanted to leave, the dinner was awkward and so again, in his words *"he took a turn to the left"* and I kept questioning what the hell did he mean by that and, smiling he said he told her: *"So let's get the check, and go to the hotel"*; she got offended. Told him she wasn't "that kind of girl." She thought it was a real date. She thought she was with a single man.

She didn't know she was on a date with someone who had a fiancée – and if you ever read this book, I am so sorry you even wasted your time with someone so low. Unfortunately, I spent nine years.

He claimed he just dropped her off and didn't stay at the hotel. But the screenshot said otherwise, it was a Booking.com review request sent to his email. And hotels don't ask for reviews if you never check in… or do they? But I was still blind, remember? So even after learning yet another awful truth, I kept holding on.

One day during the almost professionally scheduled dates, he suggested we go out on the jet skis the next day – and I didn't want to, I didn't have energy and I told him it felt forced and if that was the case I rather just stay in my house.

I would just sleep away with the Xanax and wait for the weekend to be over.

Then came the bombshell. That's when he appreciated my understanding and decided to confess some of the "demons" he battled and came forward stating he had a porn addiction, that he had been watching porn all day, every day, at work, in the car, in the bathroom. It had consumed him. He had multiple email addresses with multiple subscriptions. It was an addiction. It desensitized him. He said it distorted his ability to connect with real intimacy.

When I heard that, all I could think about was Valentine's Day. I gifted him a sex box so we could have some fun together as I am all about fun stuff. I had already purchased the erotic Jenga and the 365 sex positions cards so we could do one position a day, having sex all year around – never once he had the curiosity to play.

Back to the sex box, it was a playful, a wild gift filled with new toys: a whip, feathers, a plug, lube, lingerie… everything meant to make things exciting and adventurous. I've always been open, loose, and fun in bed, but as I mentioned in previous chapters, he often made things awkward anytime I leaned into something more sexual, wild. But that part of me, I had already reclaimed. Still, I wanted to please him. I wanted to reconnect. To be both his fantasy and his safe place.

He didn't even want to open the box.

Because by then, I wasn't enough. No one real ever is to someone trapped in that kind of addiction.

But it didn't stop there.

He admitted that the erratic behavior started before our engagement. He started frequenting strip clubs as if it was a trip to a supermarket. I asked him, "How? When?"

As he described, it started with visits to strip clubs. He would sneak out during the day while I was at work, or sometimes after leaving his own job, before coming home, or when I traveled with my family. He said it began small, just visits at first, but it escalated. Over time, it became full-blown, and he eventually confessed to sleeping with countless strippers. While I was focused on growth and building our future, working hard, he was using our money to throw dollar bills at women and buy sex. So pitiful.

The same man who scolded me for spending money on trips. The same man who made me feel guilty for wanting new clothes or dreaming about a vacation. The same man who blamed me for the broken AC or the wedding debt. That man was sneaking out to pay for sex, and I had no idea. It's almost as if having a strong, independent woman next to him made him feel small, while prostitutes and low-class women made him feel like a great catch. Well, if he chose to lower his standards… I chose to raise my bar.

He would come home like everything was fine. And I, like a fool, would cook, clean, love him, rub his back, forgive his coldness, pick up after him, load the dishwasher... all of it. How idiotic of me, especially after the comment he made in Turks and Caicos. It's disturbing, the things your mind can convince you to accept. But I'm grateful I found the root cause. And I'm certain: I will never let anyone do me wrong like that again.

And then there was the condo sticker on his car. I mentioned it once in the wedding chapter, but it needs to be emphasized here again. That sticker haunted me. It was from a place I didn't recognize. I asked him multiple times, *"Where is this from?"* He claimed he didn't know. But he remembered every minor inconvenience I ever caused him, every time I was "too emotional," every dollar I ever spent (my own money), every dinner I wanted, every person I ever texted. But he didn't know where a giant condo sticker on his car came from? How convenient.

No. He knew. He just didn't want to admit it. Because that sticker was evidence of a double life, or maybe even a triple life, considering he was having an affair with the prostitute. And despite all of this, despite every lie, every betrayal, I still tried to make it work. And I must say nowadays, how fucking stupid was I. That's how deep in the fog I was. That's what codependency does.

I told him, *"Let's put it all behind us. Let's forgive everything. It's all part of the bundle, and everything that happened before today will be forgiven. Clean slate."* He agreed, but nothing changed.

The words were there, but the effort wasn't. I was ready to start over, wholeheartedly. I had hope. I believed that if we could both let go of the past, we might finally have a chance. But while I was ready to rebuild, he was already checked out. Emotionally absent. Physically unavailable. Energetically gone.

I had to start "scheduling appointments" just to see him. Like a meeting. Like a task on his to-do list. If I didn't "earn" time with him, by being calm enough, loving enough, undemanding enough, I didn't get it. There was no spontaneity. No effort.

No desire to actually be around me. He'd say, *"We'll see each other tomorrow"* and I'd hold onto those words like a lifeline. But almost every time, he'd cancel last minute. *"Too many things to do." "Too tired." "Something came up."* The excuses came like clockwork, polite, robotic, rehearsed. He always sounded just busy enough. Just exhausted enough. Just out of reach.

And I? I was left pacing, overthinking, shrinking. Trying to be more patient. Less needy. More understanding. More "chill." Like I was trying to win a man who was already mine. My anxiety skyrocketed. I'd sit by the phone, waiting for the text or call that might change everything… or nothing at all. I started to dread the quiet. The silence between us grew louder than any fight. And I was too ashamed to admit I was still holding on to someone who kept pushing me away, so I internalized the blame.

Maybe I was too much. Maybe I hadn't really forgiven everything. Maybe I didn't deserve the clean slate I offered. But the truth was simpler and sadder: I was ready to heal, and he was never planning to meet me there. I never knew if I would see him. I never knew if I'd be rejected. I never knew what version of him I would get.

And I was stuck, scared to make plans with someone else, scared to book a trip, scared to do anything that might ruin the tiny chance that he might call, and I wouldn't be available. Meanwhile, he always knew exactly where I was, what I was doing, who I was talking to. He had full control. And I was isolated, again. But this time... I had handed him the tools. I had let him in. I had allowed it. And that's what hurt the most.

Then, unfortunately, we found out one of our dogs, had cancer, and didn't have much time left. He told me we'd take the dogs out over the weekend, maybe go to the beach, just spend time with them. But he procrastinated. None of those plans ever happened – It was Mother's Day weekend.

He invited me to his mom's house for lunch, and I went. My own mother was in Brazil at the time, and I wasn't speaking with her. Me, my sister and my brother sent our mother a breakfast basket in Brazil, and I sent flowers to his mom, to thank her for all the support she'd been giving me.

He made a sweet gesture, and had flowers delivered to my house. And once again, I thought we were getting back on track.

But it was performative.

Like a calculated deposit into the emotional bank account, so he could withdraw ten times more without guilt.

That afternoon, I laid on his lap at his house. For the first time in weeks, I felt safe. I told him I was going to order Taco Bell and asked if he wanted anything.

He said, "Don't order anything. We're going out to dinner."

Surprise.

A thoughtful gesture.

He even arranged for my son to meet us. It was beautiful.

But it was textbook.

The same narcissistic cycle, idealization, devaluation, discard. Repeat.

The next day, I couldn't eat. I couldn't work. I couldn't breathe.

My friend said something that stuck with me:

"It's like you're in the eye of a storm and you can't see anything. You've got foggy glasses on. Everything's spinning."

That was exactly how it felt.

So, I acted. I put in for time off work, didn't tell anyone what was happening other than my son and my therapist. I needed to check myself into a mental health clinic, disconnect. I told her to only notify him I was there after I was already admitted.

I paid out of pocket and spent a week at the clinic, and while I was there… I healed. Or at least, I thought I did. While I was in treatment, we arranged for me to continue seeing my private therapist daily for one hour. One of those days each week was reserved for couples therapy, an hour and a half. It felt structured, safe, empowering. I was doing the work. I was showing up for myself in ways **I never had before.**

I felt strong. I felt confident. So much that I went into the couple's session ready to draw the line. I told him: *"You're either all in, or all out"*. Because the way he was handling things, this half-in, half-out limbo, was not helping me. But deep down, I was lying. To myself. To my therapist. To him. It was my ego. My pride. I wanted him to fight for me. To chase me. To be afraid to lose me.

He cried. Cried as if someone had just told him I'd died. And for a moment, it felt real. Like he finally saw what he was about to lose. I hung up from that call thinking I was doing fantastic. That I had finally put an end to it. That I was done. But I wasn't. Not yet.

While I was in the clinic, they had me on antidepressants, anti-anxiety medication, and even medication to stimulate my appetite. But two days before I was discharged, I was also prescribed sertraline, an SSRI commonly used for depression and anxiety. But what most people don't realize, and what no one warned me about, is that for some individuals, it can make things worse before they get better. Studies have shown that sertraline, like other SSRIs, can cause intense side effects in certain people: agitation, restlessness, insomnia, even increased suicidal thoughts, especially in the first few weeks. And I felt all of it. My thoughts became faster, darker, more obsessive. I wasn't sleeping. I couldn't sit still. It was like my brain had been lit on fire, and no one around me seemed to notice that I was burning. At first, I felt fine.

I was even making plans, excited to finally feel a bit "normal" again.

A week after I left the clinic, something inside me had changed, but I did not realize it could have been my medicine combo and continued with it.

That Friday, my cousin was in town from Brazil. My brother and his girlfriend were around too. We made plans to go Friday for dinner in Miami, go on a boat ride on Saturday, and then a night out at Marion. It all felt light. Exciting. Like maybe I was finding my way back.

But when Friday came, the anxiety started bubbling. Quietly at first, then stronger. And by the end of the day, I could feel the darkness creeping back in. The suicidal ideation I thought I had left behind was back, silent, sharp, and terrifying. I confessed those feelings to my therapist, Paula, and she quickly called me and stayed on the phone with me until I was with my cousin, she wanted to make sure I was safe and didn't do anything tragic.

I hadn't spoken to him since that last couples therapy session. The one where I told myself I was done. Where I thought I had closed the chapter. But now, I realized... I hadn't. Because if I had, I wouldn't be unraveling like this.

On Saturday, we went on the boat as planned. At first, it was beautiful, sunlight, music, drinks, laughter. But then I noticed a couple on board who had recently gotten married. They talked about it constantly, about the love. And I should have seen it for what it was: a trigger. I should have removed myself, jumped in the water, changed the subject, anything. But I didn't. I sat there and listened. And the tension grew.

That night, we went to Marion. I looked amazing. I was dressed to kill, trying to hold it all together, trying to fake that I was okay. And then, when I least expected it, a bachelorette party exploded right behind me. The kind of celebration I had imagined for myself not long ago. The kind I had lost. And in that moment, everything caved in.

I went out into the world thinking I was ready. But I quickly learned I had more triggers than I ever imagined. People were talking about marriages, engagements, bachelorette parties happening all around me, and that's when I realized: I wasn't healed. I was far from healed. And that's when I absolutely lost myself.

On Sunday, June 8th, I pulled out my huge bag of medications to take my scheduled pills, and in that moment, it hit me. He was killing me slowly. Not with his hands, but with the damage, the chaos, the emotional destruction he left in his wake. I looked at the bag. At the pills. And I realized I couldn't do this anymore. I took a picture of the bag and sent it to him. I said I was over living and that I couldn't keep going like this.

He talked to me. Calmed me down. Pulled me back from the edge I felt I was about to jump from.

Then came Monday, June 9th. I tried to work, tried to show up for myself. But I could barely function. I stared at my screen, disconnected, barely able to get anything done. The day was literal hell. I kept telling my therapist that I was ready to let go of life. The more I tried to recover, the lower I was pushed. It felt like every step forward was followed by a landslide backward. She advised that I should never be left alone. But I was alone.

That day, I left work early. By noon, I couldn't function, I was spiraling. I called him, and we met at a gas station. He asked me to get into his car but me, being smart, and knowing the emotional traps I'd fallen into before, I refused. I told him he could come to my car. He was agitated, impatient, barely present. Meanwhile, I was inching closer and closer to ending it all. To just… stop the pain.

Later that day, I drove to the beach. I needed to see the water, to sit beneath the moon, to wait until midnight. June 10th would've marked our ninth anniversary. The plan was simple, in the most tragic way: take a handful of the strong pills I'd been prescribed. Drift away. Fall asleep and never wake up.

That night, both, him and my therapist were concerned. I finally disclosed my location. He came. He said everything I wanted to hear. And of course, I wasn't thinking clear, my mind wasn't safe. But even then, in that fragile moment, he still made it about himself. He wanted to go home. I told him I had nowhere to go. And what did he offer? A hotel room.

A hotel room? Like, excuse me? What did he think I would do if I went to our old house? Spend the night wrapped in memories and come out healed? He asked me to promise I'd go home, and at that point, I would've said anything anyone wanted to hear, just to be left alone. Just so I could finally do what I wanted.

But fortunately… I'm a woman who can't lie, and I did go home.

June 10th, 2025

At some point during couples therapy, he had promised we'd do something special for our anniversary. He said he would only work half the day so we could spend it together. But, as I should've predicted, he worked all day. That morning, he sent me some food, an effort to get me to eat, since I had barely been eating at all. Later that day, he had a bouquet of lilies delivered. Lilies, but somehow, they felt empty that day. That was his idea of "something special." A delivered lunch, a bouquet of lilies and one hour with me - on the clock, literally. That was the anniversary he gave me. That was the value he placed on our relationship. I loved the lilies, but even then, I questioned it.

Why lilies? Why not red roses, like he always used to get me?

He said it was late in the day and they were the only ones available, convenient. Anniversary dates don't happen unpredictably, that just showed me he had nothing planned, nor cared to put any effort.

That day, I laid on his chest. And when he noticed I was on the verge of a panic attack, he tried to calm me down. He kissed me goodbye and left.

Just like that.

The days that followed were hell.

I wanted to end everything.

I ran, from my family, from him, from everyone.

At some point in one of those conversations with him, I can't even remember the exact order because that entire week was fueled by chaos and trauma, he finally admitted a few things that left me speechless.

After all this time, he confessed that my instinct had been right all along. He admitted to having flirtatious conversations with the IV girl from the clinic, the same one I had questioned him about before. He swore that nothing physical ever happened, but the fact that he finally acknowledged the inappropriate connection, after months of gaslighting and denying, was both validating and devastating.

He also claimed that he was now disgusted by strip clubs, that he wanted nothing to do with it anymore. But knowing his patterns, I strongly doubted that was true. It felt like just another temporary performance, another empty promise. And in the midst of all that, during one of our conversations, he had the audacity to say that women nowadays are terrible, that they're all whores. The irony was suffocating.

The same man who had lied, cheated, humiliated, and broken me, now blaming women for the decay of morality. It was almost laughable, if it hadn't been so infuriating.

He told me that yes, he and the prostitute had talked about a visa and she had quickly suggested that marriage would be the fastest route, hinting at it without hesitation.

He claimed that's where the conversation ended, and that he had no intention of revisiting it. He also confessed that he ended things with her the day after my birthday, which suddenly explained the emails I received from her on Christmas Eve. She mocked me, saying I had "bigger horns than the deer he hunted." She taunted that I didn't even know what he whispered when they made love. Mind you, he's completely silent when he makes love. I'm the one who talks dirty.

He told me he didn't love her. Didn't even care about her. She was just something to fill a void, a temporary escape from the life he had built with me. He said he didn't realize how deep he was in the mess until it was too late. Until he was in too deep to climb out. He got caught up in the lies, the fantasy, the double life, and when it all came crashing down, he had no idea how to fix it.

I suppose he was afraid she would eventually tell me everything. And she did. She exposed the truth. But to him, she wasn't real. She lived in another country. It felt like a fantasy that couldn't touch him. In the end, they were using each other. She was chasing her American dream. He was running from responsibility, hiding in a world where no one expected anything of him.

And remember that big teddy bear he once carried all the way from the gate to my house? I burned it. Right there in the fire pit in our backyard before I flew to Colombia. After seeing the card that read "TQM, Tu Osito", I knew I never wanted anything to do with teddy bears ever again.

June 11th, 2025

I went to work, pretending like I could keep it together. But I was spinning. Slowly, and then all at once. I was spiraling again, only this time, it felt different. Darker. Heavier. Like the pain had sunk into my bones. At one point, I called my parents, my therapist, and him, and told them I didn't want to live anymore. There was no filter. No pretense. Just raw, unbearable honesty. I said the words out loud: "I don't want to be here."

Then I messaged my boss. She sensed something was wrong and called me. I apologized through tears. I told her I was suicidal and that I was exhausted from living in the darkness. I also told her, that no matter how hard I tried, I couldn't find the light. She listened. She stayed calm. And she saved my life.

I told her I was going out for a drive, to clear my head. She didn't believe me. She contacted someone at work and told them to come find me, but I had already left. Then I got a call from a therapist from a program at work, and I said I was fine. But that wasn't the truth.

Next thing I know, my father showed up at my workplace, he said he wasn't leaving until I came outside and talked to him. I thought it was just a conversation, a moment of concern. I drove back but it was a trap. A well-meaning one, but still, a trap.

He got in the car with me and said, *"I'm not leaving your side anymore."*

That was the moment I broke. I was furious, not because he didn't care, but because he cared too late.

Because in that moment, I didn't want to be saved, I wanted to disappear.

I drove us both home fighting, saying horrible things and told him he would seal my casket.

My father, determined to protect me, told my mother to not leave my side.

She stayed with me, sweet, innocent, unaware.

And then…I said horrible things to her, every distorted perception I had was suddenly my family's responsibility. Then I started popping pills.

Right in front of her.

She didn't understand. She thought they were my supplements, the ones prescribed to help me eat again. She looked at me, confused, and asked gently, "Is that the one to help your appetite?" And I smiled. A haunting, hollow smile. And I said, "No. I'm killing myself right in front of you, and you haven't even realized." It shattered her. The horror in her eyes, the disbelief, it all happened in slow motion.

Moments later, the police were at my door. EMTs. Sirens. Uniforms. Flashing lights. They told me I was being Baker Acted and that I was going to be taken to a facility involuntarily. They stated that I was a danger to myself.

In that moment, I tried to explain that I wasn't doing anything, that they misunderstood me and that it was a moment of weakness, nothing to worry as I was now safe, at home. But it was too late.

I gave them my husband's number, thinking he would protect me. Surely, he will tell them I don't need to be taken and that I'm okay, I just needed to rest. After all, he had told me time and time again: *"I would never put you in harm's way."* But when they called him, he didn't even hesitate and told them to take me. Involuntarily. No compassion. Just compliance.

That betrayal cut deeper than any blade could. Because in that moment, I wasn't his wife. I wasn't someone to protect. I was just… an inconvenience. A problem to be handed off to someone else. And for the second time in less than a year, I was being locked away. Not because I was violent, not because I was unstable. But because I was broken… and no one wanted to hold the pieces.

They put me in the back of an ambulance and took me, my second trip around the drain.

As they headed towards the hospital, I saw his car, chasing the ambulance. When I arrived at the hospital, the first thing I did was invoke my rights under HIPAA, making it clear that I did not authorize anyone to be informed of my condition.

I was furious about what had just happened, furious that they had taken me against my will.

Quite honestly, before the EMTs even got to me, I had already stacked medication into my pockets. I knew the process: once I arrived, they'd make me change into a gown. So, upon arrival, I hid the pill card under the hospital sheets, along with my vape and my phone. As expected, they told me to undress and assigned me a sitter. They turned off the lights in the room, and she was too busy scrolling through her phone to notice anything. So, I covered my head under the blanket and, without hesitation, continued popping pills, vaping and texting, until the medication finally sedated me completely.

When I was declared medically stable, they transferred me to a facility I won't name here for obvious legal reasons. But let me be clear: they treated me like a dog in a kennel. How in the world can someone who is facing a mental breakdown be taken to a place that makes them feel even worse? In my 24 hours there, they refused to give me my medication, locked the rooms so we had to sit in the hallways or in a small glass room where they could watch us like rats in a cage. If we wanted a water, we had to ask permission for them to unlock a door.

If you know me, you know I wasn't settling for that. I called 911 myself and demanded proper care. Paramedics were dispatched. I told them they weren't giving me the medication I needed, and I still hadn't seen a psychiatrist, just an ARNP through an iPad. I insisted on speaking with a doctor, and they assured me that it would be the first order of business the next morning.

Well, no. The doctor never came. Instead, they gave me another iPad consult. Thankfully, I was finally able to explain everything that had happened. Based on my condition and explanation, the Baker Act was lifted, as it was not warranted. I had been speaking erratically, but I did not pose a threat to myself, I was simply taking my prescribed medication.

I was livid at my family for putting me there. I called my ex-husband and told him I'd be released the next day, and that he'd have to help me, whether by letting me stay in the guest bedroom, getting me a short-term Airbnb, or helping me figure something out. And that's exactly what I did. I left the clinic, took an Uber to retrieve my car, and drove straight to his house.

I tried calling him a few times, but I knew Fridays were usually his busiest days, so I texted instead. I wrote: *"Hey, I opened the garage and came inside. I haven't slept or showered in three days, so I'll do that while I wait for you."* He called me immediately and, with a cold tone, asked me to respectfully wait in my car. By then, I had already walked into the house and that's when I noticed a few things:

One, he continued to hide all my belongings in drawers and closets, as if there was no sign of me in the house.

Second, I went to use the restroom and realized there was toilet paper in the trash folded like a rose, the kind cleaning ladies usually do, it was odd, as the rest of the house was dirty, as usual. He is filthy and no matter how much I cleaned the house, between the dog hair, his messy behavior and his IBS condition ruining the toilets, it was always nasty. I honestly never had people over because I was embarrassed.

Then, third, I saw the spare bedroom bed was messy, as if someone had slept on it. Considering we had an aggressive dog; I knew immediately what that meant, he must've had someone over and locked the dog in the master bedroom. I also noticed a single rose on the kitchen counter, stuffed into a water bottle.

Still, I respected his request. I walked back to my car, pulled it halfway into the garage for shade as I hadn't eaten in seven days, and I was too weak to sit under the sun.

Then he arrived.

He marched into the garage with the same friend I had described before, the pawn, the one who followed him blindly, always loyal, always available, despite being constantly belittled and disrespected. His trained dog. His echo. His enabler. They both walked in, and he, without hesitation, locked the garage door behind them. Then he circled around to the front entrance, came up to my car, and delivered the coldest words I've ever heard:

"Number one, please back out of the garage" – and so I did.

Then he walks to my car window and says:

"Second, I need you to leave, I don't want you to get in trouble, I already called the police."

Wait, what? Now I was livid, fuming. I tried to back my car out of the garage, fully decided that this time, I was going to go through with it. In a quick move, he then opened the door and told me I wasn't leaving. A complete contradiction, he told me I had to leave, had just called the police on me, and now suddenly I wasn't allowed to leave?

I was able to get back in my car, close and lock the door, then drove off, furious and devastated. I parked my car near Delray Beach. I sat there for hours, staring at the ocean, waiting for the day to end. I had just been Baker Acted. I felt like my family had turned against me, and now the one person who promised to protect me had humiliated me, treated me like an intruder, and discarded me like trash, again! I was done.

I made up my mind, this time I was going to go in peace. We went back and forth on the phone, and slowly, he started breadcrumbing again.

When I mentioned the rose, I had seen on his kitchen counter, he turned it into some grand emotional metaphor. He said the rose somehow represented me.

He begins to tell the tale that when he got back to his car after I was taken to the hospital, he noticed all cars in the parking lot had a sunflower on the windshield, except his. His had a rose. He told me he got angry, threw the rose, cried, and regretted not getting me red roses like he used to.

He then said he picked the rose back up and prayed, like he had never done before hoping I was okay. It was classic, just enough sentiment to keep me hooked, just enough drama to make me feel chosen, while still doing absolutely nothing meaningful.

I gave him my location, and as I expected, he didn't show up. Instead, he facetimed me and told me to go get a hotel or just go home, except I couldn't drive, I had already taken my prescribed medication and eventually started to drift off. I think he must have called again and, when I didn't answer, he decided to come find me.

When he arrived, he wasn't calm. He was aggressive, furious, loud voice, screaming. He threatened to hog-tie me and throw me in the back of his truck.

That was when I panicked and for the first time, I actually got scared of him. I quickly jumped to the driver's seat and told him I'd go to a hotel, anything to get away from him. And once again, he left me. Alone. I nearly crashed head-on with another vehicle on the way to the hotel, so, I decided I'd go home and continue destroying myself there.

The next day he said he would come over speak with me and with my father regarding both of us going to a clinic together in Brazil, but I was in auto destruction mode.

I ordered a bottle of champagne, asked to have it delivered out back on my room's window and sent him a video of me drinking. He texted my father questioning why they were allowing me to drink and why did I still have my car keys?

My father was furious and notified me he was no longer coming.

That's when I tried calling him, and he refused to pick up my calls. I jumped in my car and started driving to his house and by the time I got there, I noticed he wasn't home.

I was at my lowest, distraught and broken, not knowing who to turn to anymore so I called his father crying.

The apple doesn't fall far from the tree.

I told him I wanted to die. That I was lost. That I couldn't breathe.

And his response?

"Oh, that's stupid, just take a step back and relax. I'd love to continue talking to you, but I must walk into dinner."

I was shocked, but not really.

It just showed me how bad my ex-husband's upbringing truly was.

I then called my mother and asked her to call my ex-husband and have him call me back, she refused.

I blamed my family for everything that was unfolding since they called the police, and I was so distraught and in such a dark place that I told her they'd find my body on his driveway.

I reminded her that I had already done it once, and I could do it again. She fainted.

I heard my father in the background in panic, screaming at my sister for help so they could rush my mother to the hospital.

When I called again, the phone was on speaker. My father was upset, but she heard my voice on the background and started to come around.

I promised her I'd come home, that I had no intention to do anything and that I would let her sleep with me like she had asked before.

I got home, comforted her, and that's when everything cracked open. She cried and told me she wasn't young anymore, but she would help me get through this no matter what. What she said next, shattered me: *"If I die, I want to be cremated and thrown in the trash."*

That was the moment I realized how deeply I had hurt her. She wasn't my enemy. She was broken too, watching her daughter fall apart and feeling completely helpless. And all she wanted... was for me to survive.

Meanwhile, on my ex-husband's end, the silent treatment had started. He said he wouldn't talk to me again until I agreed to return to mental health facility, the one he asked me not to go before, to treat the very thing he had helped destroy.

That's when something finally clicked. I finally stopped and thought to myself: Alright, let's see if this man is truly worried about my wellbeing, or if he's just scared, I'll die, and he'll be held accountable. So, I told him I would go back to the clinic the following day, and asked if he was willing to pay for it. I got no response, but I was decided I was going in regardless.

I went to see Barbara G., the very same friend who had tried to warn me from the beginning. And the moment I saw her, it was like something cracked open inside me. She didn't hold back. She looked me in the eyes crying, and asked:

"Do you even love him that much? Or is this just tough Gabby trying to win, trying to prove a point for your pride and your ego?"

Her words hit me hard. Then, through tears, she said:

"No matter what, I'm here. You don't have to do this alone. Come live with me. We'll get out of this together."

And then she reminded me of something I had buried deep:

"Do you remember our picture, sitting on the sand the day of your wedding welcome party?" I nodded.

"Do you remember what you told me that day?" she asked.

I said no. And then she said it, words I'll never forget:

"You told me you didn't know what you were doing. That you weren't even sure you wanted it. But you were doing it anyway."

In that moment, everything shifted. I realized I had been screaming *"help"* for so long, just no one had heard me through the smile.

The next morning, I sent him a photo of myself, pale, lifeless, looking like a corpse, 9 days without any food, just water and a vape. Along with it, I wrote:
"I used to be beautiful. This is what your destruction has done to me."

Only then did he respond. He said "okay" and added that he was happy I was getting help. I told him I was arranging everything to be admitted the next day, and that the clinic would be contacting him for payment. I clearly stated that the two-week stay would cost $13,000. He agreed.

I moved forward, confirmed my spot, and let the clinic know he would be the point of contact for payment, and that's when he showed his true intentions.

When they called, he told them there had been a change in plans and that my father would be handling payment instead. Now mind you, it wasn't about the money; it was about emotional responsibility. About human decency. The least he could've done was pick up the phone, call my family, and say: *"Here's what the clinic costs. I can help with part of it, or I can't at all, but what can we do to support her together?"* But no. That wasn't in his nature. His only priority was dropping me off and washing his hands of the situation.

Later, he tried to justify it by saying it didn't matter who paid. And maybe it didn't. But what mattered was his complete lack of character. Even if he couldn't contribute financially, despite knowing he could, he didn't even try. That moment showed me everything. I had spent so long convincing myself that he was a good person who made bad choices. But this? This was clarity. He wasn't just someone who did bad things, he was a **bad person**. And all those moments that once felt like love? They were just performances, rehearsed for the sake of his own image, his own comfort, his **own self-preservation.**

The world has a way of spinning back around and slapping you right in the face. That's exactly how it felt. I couldn't bring myself to let my parents shoulder the financial burden alone, especially not for something that was a direct result of his actions. His betrayals, his lies, his emotional destruction. He had shattered my mental health, had left me with the wedding debt, but the cost of picking up those pieces was now falling on the shoulders of the people who had always loved me unconditionally. That didn't sit right with me. And then I remembered I knew the owner of the clinic.

Without hesitation, I reached out to my dear friend, Castro, who would do absolutely anything to see me happy, who had always shown up for me. I explained everything: I needed immediate help, that it had been nine days since I had eaten a single bite of food, that I was surviving on nothing but water, pills and vape. I told him I didn't know how much longer I could hold on, and I needed him to intervene.

Without missing a beat, he acted. Within ten minutes, he had contacted our mutual friend, the clinic's owner, and arranged a full scholarship for me. Ten minutes. That's all it took for someone who actually cared to step up and do what needed to be done. No drama, no guilt trips, no conditions. Just compassion.

I was admitted the same day, after nine full days without food, and barely enough strength to walk through the doors. The moment I arrived; the clinical team got to work. They took one look at me and knew something was deeply wrong. Through careful evaluation, they discovered that the combination of medications I had been prescribed was worsening everything. The mix was known to increase suicidal ideation, trigger aggression, and deepen depression. No wonder I had felt so lost, so hopeless, so utterly consumed by darkness.

For the first time in weeks, I didn't feel crazy.

I felt seen.

I felt understood.

And most importantly, I finally felt like I had a real chance to survive.

While at the clinic, I learned that a boundary without consequence is nothing more than a suggestion and I had to learn it the hard way. Every time I laid down a line and allowed it to be crossed without action, I was teaching him that my limits were flexible, that my pain was weightless, my words carried no follow-through.

I thought I was loving him by being patient, by forgiving endlessly, by offering chance after chance, but what I was really doing was giving him full permission to keep disrespecting me.

Every time I chose understanding over self-respect, I chipped away at my own worth. And it took being broken, completely, devastatingly broken, before I finally understood: a boundary only has real power when you're willing to walk away when it's crossed. Otherwise, it's just noise.

During my stay, everything began to shift. I started reading, devouring every piece of information I could about codependency, trauma bonds, emotional manipulation, and cognitive behavioral patterns.

I learned about the cycle I was trapped in, how my need to feel needed had made me tolerate the intolerable. I began understanding not just what had happened to me, but why I had allowed it. That alone was empowering.

Within just a week, paired with the right combination of medication, compassionate therapy, and self-education, I finally felt something I hadn't felt in a long time: the desire to live. Not just survive, but truly live. Even more than that, I wanted to help others. I knew I wasn't the only one walking around with invisible wounds and a heart full of shame.

One day, I noticed another patient, a man who constantly grunted, groaned, and seemed entirely disconnected from reality. He barely spoke, avoided eye contact, and seemed unreachable. But something told me to try. So, I did. I started small: tossing a volleyball around, smiling, engaging in gentle conversation. Little by little, he responded. He grunted less. He smiled once or twice. We talked. I made a joke. He laughed. Something was changing. And that was the moment I realized healing is contagious.

Sometimes, when we begin to rise, we naturally extend a hand to someone else. And seeing him begin to open showed me that my pain, my story, my experience… had value.

Then came music therapy, a session that unexpectedly moved something deep inside of me. We were asked to write down three songs: one that brought us anxiety, one that calmed us down, and one that represented a meaningful part of our life. I wrote:

"Over the Rainbow", my late uncle's favorite song. As I've shared before, I'm a spiritual person, and I receive signs from him often. That song always made me feel like he was near.

"You Are My Sunshine", the song I had been humming on the day he left for his bachelor trip. The same day I asked him not to take my sunshine away. He did anyway and gave me darkness.

"A Thousand Years", our wedding song. A song that once meant forever. Now, it carried the weight of everything I lost.

At the end of the session, all of us put our song choices into a cup. Silently, I bowed my head and whispered to my uncle: "If I'm on the right path… please show me." Our therapist began drawing, and then, goosebumps.

The first slip she pulled out was "Over the Rainbow."

My uncle's song.

I had chills from head to toe. I looked up, and in that moment, I knew. I knew I was being guided. I knew I was not alone. I knew that despite everything I had gone through, I was exactly where I needed to be. I cried, that moment, simple, silent, spiritual, was a turning point. I didn't need him. I didn't need saving. I was being supported from beyond, from within, from above.

That was the day I stopped surviving my story… and started rewriting it.

I was doing so well, hopeful, grounded, and finally starting to feel like myself again. The same client I had bonded with, the one who used to grunt constantly and barely interact, surprised me one day. He handed me a small button flower. It wasn't anything extravagant, just a simple gesture. To me it meant something. I placed the flower in my pocket and brought it back to my room. There was no water, no light, and the air conditioning made the room cold and dry. I set the little flower on top of my dresser and went to bed.

The next morning, I woke up, and the flower had bloomed.

This delicate thing, in a completely unfavorable environment, no sunlight, no nourishment, no reason to thrive, opened anyway. It was beautiful. In that moment, I knew it wasn't just a flower. It was a message. I picked it up gently, walked back to my friend, and told him, *"This flower gave me hope. It had nothing, no reason to grow, and yet it did. So, there's hope for all of us too."*

As I said, I've always been spiritual. I can feel things others don't. I sense when something is about to shift. I receive signs. While I was at the clinic, I had several vivid dreams about my uncle and my grandmother on my mother's side. I knew they were guiding me, watching over me. Reminding me I wasn't alone.

Three days later, I noticed something profound: the man who used to grunt all day long hadn't made a sound. Not one. His energy had shifted completely. I could feel it. He was lighter, calmer, and more present. I'm certain that one day soon, he'll return to the world as the incredible attorney I know he is. I had witnessed his transformation, and it mirrored mine.

By then, I felt strong. I felt ready. My family had made plans for me, and I wanted to return home. I asked to be discharged a few days early. I was in such a different place than the broken woman who had first walked through those doors, but Maricay, my therapist at the clinic, wasn't entirely comfortable with letting me go just yet. She didn't think I was ready, and I respected that. She didn't like praise but let me tell you: she's badass. A woman who saves lives every day without even realizing the weight of what she does.

So, I sat down with her and said, *"Tell me what part of me is still missing. What piece haven't I found yet? Because if you can tell me, I'll stay. I'll stay as long as you need me to."*

She looked at me and said she just wanted to know I was safe, truly safe, for one more weekend. She needed to be sure, however she suggested that if she spoke with my parents and my private therapist Paula and they all felt aligned, she would approve my discharge. I agreed and I told her, *"Whatever you decide is best for me, I'll trust it. And if you still don't think I'm ready, I promise I won't leave AMA (against medical advice). I'll sit my ass down and wait until I am."*

The next day, I got the news: I was being discharged.

She believed in me.

And what made it even more meaningful was that, in the end, she didn't need to speak with my parents or Paula. She saw it in me. She saw it in my eyes, in the way I spoke, in how I advocated for myself, not out of desperation, but from a place of clarity and strength. She believed in me, because of me. And I was so proud of that. Proud that someone who had witnessed my lowest point also witnessed my rise. She didn't discharge me because someone else vouched for me, she did it because I had earned it. Because I had finally shown up for myself in a way I never had before. That trust, that validation, that moment… it will stay with me forever.

I was ready to take back control of my life. Ready to surrender the pain. To detach from all the toxicity and the evil I had been wrapped up in. I had found myself again. The lens was finally clear. I was no longer stuck in that fog, no longer suspended in limbo. The storm my friend once described? I was no longer inside it. I was standing on the outside, watching it pass.

And I knew then, with full certainty, I didn't want anything to do with that horrible human being ever again. I had found my light, I had found me.

My farewell at the clinic was marked by a song that pierced straight through my soul, **"Rescue" by Lauren Daigle**. I had never heard it before, but the moment it played, it became my anthem of survival. I still listen to it, almost daily, as a reminder of the powerful transformation that took place within those walls. The wait for my parents, the tearful goodbyes to people who gave me nothing but unconditional love, it all felt like I was high on pure joy. If you've never heard it, I invite you to listen. Sing along. Let the words wash over you. You might feel something magical begin to move inside you, too.

Rescue – Lauren Daigle
"You are not hidden
There's never been a moment you were forgotten
You are not hopeless
Though you have been broken, your innocence stolen...
I hear you whisper underneath your breath
I hear your SOS, your SOS
I will send out an army to find you
In the middle of the darkest night
It's true, I will rescue you..."

My parents arrived with balloons in their hands, smiles on their faces, and visible relief in their eyes, they saw I was back. Back to myself.

On the drive home, they cried quietly, holding the kind of gratitude that only comes after nearly losing someone you love. They were taking me back to the place I should have never left, home. When they dropped me off at the clinic, they knew something was terribly wrong. But when they picked me up, there was no doubt, I was healed.

To highlight, during my first week there, the doctors put me back on the medications that had once worked for me, and I stabilized quickly. One thing I know for sure: I will never take an SSRI again. After this experience, and after hearing similar stories from friends, I've learned that for some of us, the side effects aren't just bad, they're dangerous.

As soon as I left the clinic, I texted Castro to thank him for everything. I also sent a message to the clinic owner, grateful for his kindness and generosity. That's when Castro revealed something that stopped me in my tracks. The person who had been quietly working behind the scenes to get me into that clinic, the helping hand I never saw, was the very person I hadn't spoken to in over two years. My former boss. The man I had once fought with and walked away from after an ultimatum that left a permanent scar. The same man my ex used as an excuse for everything he did.

My ex-husband had twisted the truth, convinced himself that I had been unfaithful with my boss. That this man was the reason for his choices. His lies. His cheating. His addiction to strip clubs. He called him a bad influence. A threat. A scapegoat. But now I know, he wasn't the problem. He wasn't the reason. The liar, the manipulator, the abuser wasn't the man I used to work for. It was the man I had married.

And yet, when my life was on the line, when I was falling apart, he showed up. Quietly. Humbly. Behind the scenes. He didn't want credit. He didn't want recognition. He just wanted me to live. That kind of kindness, the kind that asks for nothing in return, is rare. He owed me nothing yet gave me everything. He stepped in when my own husband walked away. When the man who slept next to me for nine years turned his back. When the person who promised to protect me didn't even lift a finger to help. When I needed help paying for treatment, my ex passed the cost to my parents and washed his hands clean. He walked away like it was nothing. Like he hadn't left a trail of destruction behind. He left me drowning and told me not to make waves.

That was it. That was the final click. That was the moment I realized I had spent years building a life with a man who would abandon me in my darkest hour. I didn't need more therapy to understand it. I didn't need closure. I had truth. And it was enough.

And here's a fun fact, because as I mentioned before when I was in the clinic, I had constant dreams of my uncle and my grandmother on my mother's side. Every night, they visited me. Guided me. Protected me. But the moment I was safe… the dreams stopped. They haven't come back. Not once. Because I believe they knew I was okay.

I came home from the clinic a different woman. Rebuilt. Clear. Ready. That weekend, I celebrated life. I surrounded myself with people who love me. I partied, danced, slept, laughed, rode horses. I lived again. I sat down and wrote out a list of pros and cons, clear, honest, brutal. And what I saw on paper matched what I finally saw in my heart: there was never a safe place in that relationship. There was never a future. There was only a cycle. A loop of highs and lows disguised as love.

But love shouldn't make you want to die.

Love shouldn't feel like limbo.

Love doesn't gaslight you into silence.

From now on, I choose life.

I choose me.

I began posting videos online to raise awareness about emotional abuse. I made a vow that day to use my voice, not to shame, but to save. I decided to start a nonprofit organization in Brazil to aid those who, like me, desperately needed help but couldn't afford the kind of care I was blessed to receive. I promised I would tell my story, not in sound bites, not in viral clips, but in these pages. In this book.

And every single dollar from this book…

Every bit of profit…

Will go directly to that nonprofit.

Because my story nearly ended in silence.

But I survived.

And now, I will never be quiet again.

Chapter 18: The Women Who Helped Me Rise

Healing doesn't happen in isolation. Sometimes, when your soul has been shattered and your mind is drowning in darkness, you don't crawl out of it alone. You are carried. Held. Guided. Pulled back to life by the steady hands of people strong enough to sit with your pain and remind you that you're still worthy of light.

For me, those people were Paula and Maricay.

They weren't just therapists. They were warriors. Soul mirrors. Two women who showed up when I was at my worst and never flinched. They didn't just listen, they fought for me. With their words, with their boundaries, with their presence. They met me in the mess and helped me walk through it until I could stand on my own.

Paula was the first light I reached for when everything inside me was collapsing. A woman with infinite patience and even greater strength. She didn't sugarcoat. She didn't coddle, but she held me with grace, even when I pushed her away. I was combative. I was broken. I was in the thickest fog of codependency, heartbreak, PTSD and suicidal ideation, and still, she never gave up on me.

I remember saying, repeatedly, "I can't survive this." And instead of trying to convince me otherwise with empty promises, Paula helped me see that I already was surviving it. One breath at a time.

She was the one who reminded me: I am more than one man. More than one relationship. More than one heartbreak. She helped me understand that my worth was never up for negotiation. That love doesn't have to hurt. That survival isn't the same thing as living.

She didn't just guide me, she stood beside me in every storm. Even when I brought chaos into our sessions, even when I resisted every truth she tried to show me, she never left. Her heart, full of empathy and fire, was a lifeline I didn't know I needed until I was holding on for dear life.

And then, there was Maricay.

When I was admitted to the clinic, I didn't know what to expect. I was exhausted. Drained. Hiding pills in pockets. Begging the universe to let me disappear. I had hit the bottom, and it was darker than I ever imagined.

And then she walked in, a force of nature. Real. Raw. No-nonsense. No fluff. But deeply kind. Deeply human. The kind of woman who doesn't just hand you a life raft, she jumps in the water with you and says, "We're getting out of this together."

She introduced me to the book *Codependent No More*, and with it, she helped me dismantle the illusions I had clung to for years. She made me take off my rose-colored glasses and see the truth for what it was: I was not just a victim of someone else's abuse; I was trapped in a cycle of my own distorted perceptions. My own desperate need to be loved had kept me chained to someone who didn't even deserve access to me.

With Maricay, I learned to name the enemy. Codependency. Self-betrayal. Emotional slavery. I learned that healing wasn't about hating the person who hurt me, it was about releasing the belief that I needed them to feel whole.

She was assertive, but never harsh. Empathetic, but never enabling. She balanced challenge with compassion in a way that cracked me open and poured the truth into the places I had tried so hard to numb.

And through both incredible women, I found something I hadn't felt in years:

Hope.

Hope that I could survive. That I could be more. That I could let go of the pain, the illusion, the shame, and finally, finally live.

To Paula and Maricay: you didn't just play a role in my healing. You helped save my life. You didn't walk away when I was difficult. You didn't give up when I was lost. You saw me, really saw me, when I couldn't even see myself.

You are both the reason this book exists.
And because of you, I am no longer surviving.
I am rising.

Thank you for believing I was worth saving.

I dedicate this chapter, and this part of my soul, to you both.

Forever.

Chapter 19: The War We Don't See: A Final Word on Emotional Abuse

Emotional abuse doesn't leave bruises you can see. It doesn't show up in broken bones or hospital records. It doesn't scream for attention like a black eye might. It breaks you just the same, slowly, invisibly, and often irreversibly.

It creeps in through manipulation disguised as charm. Through control dressed as care. Through gaslighting so subtle you begin to believe your feelings are the enemy.

And that's why I wrote this book.
Because people need to understand what emotional abuse really looks like. They need to know that it can happen to strong, intelligent, successful women. It can happen to women who have everything on paper, and still end up questioning if they're even worthy of love.

We don't talk about emotional abuse enough. We don't warn girls to look out for it. We teach them to watch for physical red flags, but we don't teach them how to recognize the emotional ones:

- Constant invalidation
- Withholding affection as punishment
- Making you apologize for their mistakes
- Making you feel crazy for setting boundaries
- Cheating and calling it your fault
- Refusing accountability and blaming your trauma instead

These aren't just "bad relationships." They're war zones. And the victims often don't know they're bleeding until it's almost too late.

If you're in a relationship where you're constantly questioning your worth, your reality, your sanity, you're not weak. You're being abused.

And if you're the one doing this to someone, if you're manipulating, lying, degrading, gaslighting, you're not just hurting them. You're destroying a life.

Emotional abuse is serious. It kills people. Not always with weapons. Sometimes with silence. With apathy. With abandonment in the exact moment love was needed most.

We must stop minimizing it. We must stop excusing it. We must stop letting people walk away from devastation with no consequences.

Because abusers don't just damage the women they break. They destroy everything those women could have become. The careers. The children. The friendships. The future.

And yet… we still live in a world where people say, "Well, at least he didn't hit you."

No. Enough of that.

We need awareness. We need education. We need women to speak up, and we need men to stop destroying women and walking away like nothing happened.

If this book does anything, let it be this:
Let it start conversations.
Let it validate someone who thought, they were going crazy.
Let it open eyes.
Let it save a life.

Because emotional abuse is real. It is dangerous. It is deadly.
And the war we don't see is the one most women are still silently fighting.

Not anymore.
This ends with us

www.ingramcontent.com/pod-product-compliance
Lightning Source LLC
Chambersburg PA
CBHW060459030426
42337CB00015B/1649